Empower your own back

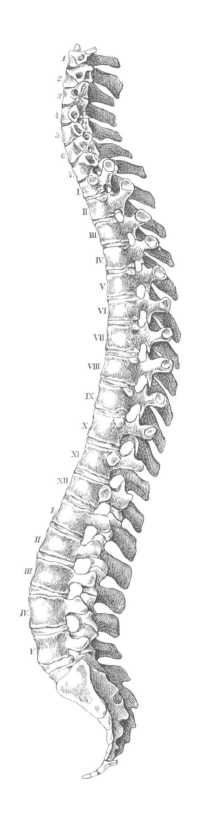

Mobility, stability,
strength, training,
palpation and self-awareness

Editorial Design: Claudio León
Illustrations: Diana Laino

Index

Jero

My training background originates from Chinese martial arts, Jiu Jitsu, Tai Chi and Chi Kung, gymnastics, wrestling and other combat sports. I always developed and continue to train something, I never stop. Formally my studies are anatomy, biomechanics and physiology, but most of my life I was self-taught in most of the aspects I developed and continue to develop.

I started training kettlebells after reading Pavel's few books that were barely available in the early 2000s. I was immediately convinced that it was my thing after following and getting right a series of practices that changed the state of my body and the way I interpreted strength and training at that time. After understanding and practising, I fell completely under the spell of kettlebells, and so strength began to be an important and decisive factor in my life. The circle began to close because I had also found a method of strength with transfer suitable for martial arts.

In the beginning I had to literally build the kettlebells in my country and for many years I travelled to different destinations around the world, the main one being the birthplace of kettlebell in St. Petersburg (Russia). I also organized visits of many foreign teachers as well as international tournaments and activities.

After these trips I created KBLA (Kettlebell Latin America) which, as its name suggests, promotes joint interests in favour of the countries that make up Latin America, prioritizing dissemination in Spanish in an accessible and even free way.

Since 2008 I have organized more than 10 international master visits, certifications and trainings on behalf of KBLA. I have also travelled to Chile, Uruguay, Paraguay, Brazil, Peru, Ecuador, Colombia, Costa Rica and the Argentinean provinces of Buenos Aires, Santa Cruz, Rio Negro, Santa Fe, Jujuy, Entre Rios, Chaco, Misiones, Mendoza, Corrientes and Cordoba. Since 2010 I have also held the first Latin American Sport Kettlebell tournaments.

In recent years I have been fully dedicated to the generation of social media content and original material such as manuals, instructional videos and online courses, specifically those on the G-SE platform, where I have developed my two courses: 'Certified Kettlebell Trainer and Fundamentals of Functional Anatomy and Movement Patterns', which have served as the basis and driving force for many of these manuals and which have then formed part of my own online training.

In the publishing world, my basic work on paper has been 'strength, training, anatomy', in which I relate these three themes to each other.

> **My goal is to try to inspire people to find their personal and unique path in fitness and movement.**

In 2021 I wrote one of my best known works, called 'The book of progressions, regressions and variants', in which I present countless examples of exercises based on movement patterns and the concept by which they can be made easier or more difficult.

In 2022 I wrote the big 'BIG3' book, a comprehensive analysis of the 3 basic exercises: squat, deadlift and bench press. This also from the perspective of strength, training and anatomy. This was followed by The book of Glutes and the present work you are holding in your hands.

I have also developed 6 free and open access works called 'Training Guides for Beginners', where the steps to get started in activities such as kettlebells, clubbells, Turkish get-up, anatomy, history and training methods are presented.

Currently, I am involved in lecturing and teaching, continuing my work to promote human movement and the more philosophical aspects of training around the world. I am dedicated to developing a model of thinking that is not absolutist, but rather relativistic, in the world of training. In this way, I seek to reinforce the importance of tailoring training methods to individual needs and circumstances, recognising that there is no single path or absolute truth in exercise and fitness.

WHAT'S THIS BOOK ABOUT?

This is not a book about spinal pain therapy or treatment. Rather, it is a guide focusing on movement, recognition and function of the spine (more specifically YOUR spine).

THIS IS NOT A BOOK TO TAKE AWAY PAIN! IT IS A BOOK TO RECOVER CAPACITIES

Although movement, strength, awareness and knowledge about a structure can contribute to the improvement of a pain or condition, these ailments are usually multifactorial and there is no direct linear relationship between a specific exercise and pain relief. While this is not a rehabilitation or pain relief book, it may help you through these processes. If in doubt, it is vital to consult and follow the advice of a specialist with whom you feel comfortable.

This book does not focus on pain.

It is a book designed to restore possibilities.

WHO IS THIS BOOK FOR?

This is my first book for the general audience.

What does this mean?
That it is a better or a worse book
compared to other audiences?

Not at all, when I say "general" it means that
this book is suitable for ALL.

For anyone who is not used to
inhabiting the world of physical
activity...

For everyone who
LIVES for and
through physical
activity...

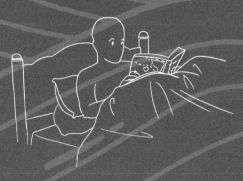

For the teacher or senior lecturer who wants to explain things in a simple way...

For the person who has never done any physical activity in their life and needs an accessible roadmap to enter this world...

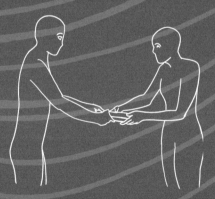

For the curious who need to understand this world explained in a simple way...

For the one who wants to help others but does not know how (this book will be a beautiful GIFT).

Your spine is yours... and as such, you have the right to reclaim all of its capabilities and functions for which it evolved and developed. However, as humans, when we lose these capacities, there is no 'claiming window' to restore them to us. The reality is that, except in cases of genetic or developmental conditions, or due to an unfortunate accident, it is we who are responsible for the current condition of our spine.

The book you hold in your hands focuses on how to try to recover, maintain or maximise these inherent capacities of your spine.

This is not a book of tricks or hacks for your spine, but a guide to EMPOWERMENT. To achieve this goal, we first have to accept and take responsibility that the current situation (good or bad) of our spine is the result of our accumulated actions (or lack thereof) throughout our lives. This may sound uncomfortable, but it will be the first necessary step in taking control of your destiny.

EXCEPT IN SPECIAL SITUATIONS,
YOU ARE PRIMARILY
RESPONSIBLE FOR THE
SITUATION OF YOUR SPINE.

DEPENDING ON HOW WE LOOK
AT IT, WE CAN TAKE THIS AS A
NEGATIVE OR AS A POSITIVE.

BUT IT IS IMPORTANT TO
UNDERSTAND THAT WE ARE,
TO A CERTAIN EXTENT, THE
ARCHITECTS OF OUR OWN
DESTINY.

If you bought this book expecting 'the book' itself to solve your problems, it is time to close it and give it a more useful purpose, as a PC monitor stand or paperweight. The real purpose of this book is to serve as a map, which, through your DESIRE, WILL AND DISCIPLINE will guide you towards greater autonomy and care of your spine.

IS NOT A TREATMENT BOOK OR A BOOK OF MAGIC FORMULAS. IT IS A BOOK DESIGNED TO EMPOWER YOU, THROUGH KNOWLEDGE, TO BE ABLE TO GUIDE YOUR SPINE TO REACH ITS FULL POTENTIAL.

To know and connect with your spine, it is not necessary to memorise names and complicated structures. While this knowledge is valuable, often the deepest understanding comes through sensation and perception of your parts. However, consider that the more resources you add to your 'toolbox', the more perspectives and possibilities you will gain.

This way, depending on your personality type and preferences, you will be able to connect better:

- Through images and visualizations.
- Through theory and written descriptions.
- Through practice and movement.
- Through logic and judgement.

We must understand that each person will have a greater or lesser affinity with these proposals, as if they were a flavour of ice cream, and all of them will be valid!

The spine is a complex structure and, architecturally, it is STILL DEBATED whether it is perfect, having had to overcome numerous obstacles throughout evolution and daily life. It is so difficult to understand its structure and function that this book has been perhaps the most difficult for me to write, given the task of translating the complexity of the spine into simple and understandable words.

Therefore, the idea of this book is that you first understand the function and structure of the spine. To become familiar with it through palpation, touch and visualization. To regain its mobility and, very importantly, to understand that mobility without support, structure or strength is as useless as a car without an engine.

With this in mind, I have organized some exercises in a progressive manner so that you can simply and effectively build a good base of mobility and combined strength.

I repeat: what you have in your hands is a book to increase your knowledge about this structure of your body: the spine. This is not a treatment book, nor does it contain magic formulas such as 'do this stretch to cure the back pain'.

We must understand that each person is unique and you cannot assess, diagnose, let alone recommend a type of exercise from a book without knowing the person. So please don't try to link an exercise to a specific ailment... because in most cases it simply won't work.

If you are experiencing a reduction in the capabilities of your spine or are suffering from pain, I would recommend that you see a professional to specifically address your condition. If you think you already have the tools you need to move forward, then you can put this book aside and start now, and if you don't, don't dismiss it and read on!

Each person is a different world, we cannot apply the same concepts or techniques to everyone equally. This path begins with gaining an understanding of what your own spine is like.

Are you ready?

1

What can I do with my spine?

Regardless of whether you take a more 'creationist' perspective (believing that someone designed the spine to fulfil a specific purpose or function) or an 'evolutionist' one (considering that the spine adapted to perform certain functions), we must understand that the functions your spine fulfils are varied and important, such as:

- Protect the nervous system and act as the main highway from the brain to the periphery.

- Provide stability to the trunk.

- To transfer forces between the lower and upper limbs.

- Generate movement in all planes.

- Act as a structural axis for the ribs, head and pelvis.

- To 'shield' the posterior area of the body.

- Serve as an 'anchor' for the muscles.

- And many more aspects that we will be addressing

In order to fulfil and/or obtain all these functions, it is essential to have two basic conditions in the spine: stability and mobility.

It is important to understand that these are interdependent and not necessarily opposed. Although at first glance they may appear to be opposites, they are in fact complementary. To such an extent that even in the most formal literary terrain (such as a classical anatomy book) we find this definition of the spine: 'it must be able to move and provide support'.

That is why we will not reach the functional fullness of our spine if we do not achieve that these two conditions coexist and interact smoothly.

We need the stability of the spine to be able to fulfil the functions mentioned above, such as protection, force transfer and support.

We also require their mobility to perform functions such as movement and adaptation.

Stabilization and support   Mobility and adaptation

And how would the absence, dysfunction or decline of these conditions affect you? Unfortunately, the passage of time and/or a sedentary lifestyle can reduce these spinal capabilities. Unless you don't mind depending on someone in the future for basic tasks such as feeding or dressing, you may really WANT to maintain your spine's autonomy of movement and function, keeping its mobility and stability in optimal balance.

This conservation requires daily care, but don't worry, it doesn't necessarily imply obsessing 24 hours a day... just maintaining an attentive but relaxed concentration in your daily life. But beware, this is not something that magically manifests itself, in order to achieve and stimulate that concentration you first need to WANT to generate those daily situations.

RELAXED FOCUS

Relaxed concentration is a state of mind in which a person can fully apply his or her attention to a task without experiencing stress or excessive loss of energy.

This concept is widely trained and developed in the martial arts, where the aim is to remain calm and focused even in stressful or dangerous situations.

In this state, the mind is completely immersed in the task without distractions or worries, allowing for greater efficiency and optimal performance.

Relaxed concentration is trainable through exposure to challenging situations in a gradual and progressive way, allowing you to adapt to the difficulty in a scalable and step-by-step manner. Don't be afraid of 'danger', just try to adapt to it little by little...

**THE DESIRE IS VERY IMPORTANT, BUT SO IS THE CRITERION....
THERE ARE INTERNAL SITUATIONS (SUCH AS AN INJURY,
AN INTENSE EMOTIONAL CONDITION OR A PSYCHOLOGICAL
CONDITION) AND EXTERNAL SITUATIONS (SUCH AS THE
FAMILY ENVIRONMENT AND THE SOCIAL GROUP) THAT CAN
ACT AS BARRIERS.**

Do my....

...objectives...

...match with my actions...?

Is it the right environment?

Therefore, desire combined with judgement will allow for a proper assessment of the situation and of the actions you plan to take, which will help to reduce the number of and avoid potential frustrations.

Personally, my goal (and I believe yours) is to be or remain Self-sufficient as long as I can. This is one of the maxims by which I live and operate on a daily basis. To achieve this, we have to overcome obstacles that can cause our plan to fail and lead us to lose autonomy in our spine, such as:

- Too little physical activity
- Too much sitting or too much time on the couch
- Not specifically training the spine
- Fear of movement and strength (panic due to perceived fragility)
- Mainly due to laziness :(

At some point, this tendency is present in the majority of the world's population (you are not alone). The good news is that, just as you lose something, you can get it back:

- Increasing physical activity
- Alternate sedentary postures with dynamic ones.
- Develop specific training for your spine
- Revaluing strength.
- Desire and make a change concrete.
- Prioritise and seek relaxed concentration

The catch in this list is that many times recovering something...
is more difficult than achieving it in the first instance.
I therefore ask you to be willing to open the dialogue.
with your inner shadows and that together they will reach
to an agreement to start working...

This relationship between the fantasy of doing something, the real desire one has to do it, the possibility of doing it and the use of relaxed concentration to make it happen can be understood by analysing the theory of the 6 internal harmonies of the Chinese martial art called Hsing I. In this context, the heart, the intention and the mind are fundamental to execute an action, a plan or movement, however simple it may be:

- The heart harmonises (or directs) the intention (mind). It is the primal fire that drives us.
- The intention (mind) harmonises (or directs) the energy (Chi or bioelectricity, if you prefer a more scientific term).
- Chi harmonises (or directs) movement.

When these relationships develop harmoniously, everything seems easier, as if there is a driving force guiding us and we only need to follow a step-by-step plan to achieve our goals. However, when that driving force is missing, it is discipline that takes over. At such times, the mind must take the lead in carrying out the tasks we have set for ourselves, even when the heart or motivation is not present.

From a physical and structural point of view, the spine is the center of connection with our entire system. In order to carry out a process of recovery, maintenance or strengthening of your spine, it is necessary to have a well thought out plan. Plans always depend on the mind, but they are also fed by the energy of the heart. In the absence or decrease of one of these elements, it will be necessary to focus and increase one of them in order to achieve our goals.

The spine fulfils the
function of providing both
mobility and stability.

If we only concentrate or
worry about one of these
capacities,
we will not be realizing its
full potential.

Let us first establish: WHAT CAN YOUR SPINE DO? That is, what are its innate qualities and possibilities in a normative state of health?

Your spine can move in all directions and planes: it can tilt forward, extend backward, tilt sideways, and rotate on itself. Moreover, it can perform all these movements in combination at different heights. Thus, it could flex in the lumbar region at the same time as it bends in the dorsal region and rotates in the cervical region.

In addition to moving, your spine can stabilize itself in any of these postures or during their transitions. This means that it can be held statically, as well as stabilized dynamically.

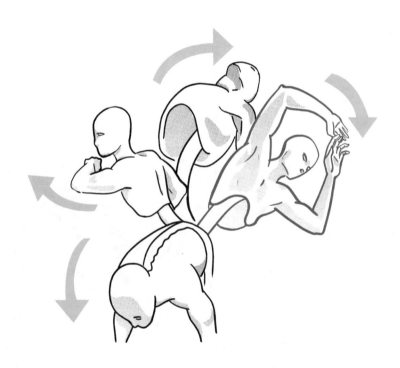

You can hold things: sometimes with very little effort, especially if the load is aligned with the line of gravity, and sometimes with greater effort, assisted by the muscles and tissues that support it. When we move the load away from our body center, we need a LOT of assistance from the muscle groups to keep it stable (this is the principle of the categorization called 'core training').

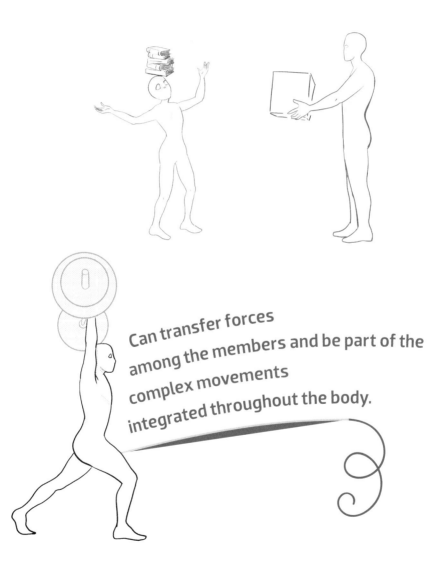

Can transfer forces among the members and be part of the complex movements integrated throughout the body.

Your spine is a multi-planar tool; not only can it align with all planes, but it can also easily switch from one to another and operate in several planes at the same time.

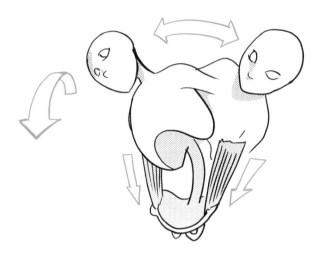

WHY NOT START BY STRETCHING?

Stretching as a treatment and training approach for the spine is currently overrated.

The ability to stretch an area of the body is not necessarily an indicator of health or a guarantee against pain. You may be able to easily touch your toes with your hands, but that doesn't mean you won't suffer from back pain.

Or you may be able to reach just below the knees and experience no pain at all. The amount of stretch is not a real parameter of health, but it can be a limiting factor in your body's range of motion, especially if you seek to express yourself in all planes, vectors and ranges of motion.

THE SPINE CAN BE MOBILIZED TO:

- Increase movement possibilities: reaching, stretching, lifting, etc.

- Maintain joint lubrication

- Stimulate circulation in the surrounding structures

- Relieve mental stress

- Feel lighter

THE SPINE CAN BE STRENGTHENING TO:

- Be more efficient: By being stronger, everything requires less effort

- To be more confident in our body structure

- Have a 'safety belt' for real life situations: falls, crashes, blows and external aggressions.

- Interacting with external forces

- Applying external force, e.g. when moving something heavy.

Based on the above, I can present you with a dilemma that has plagued human beings for the last decades: Should I 'stretch' my spine or should I 'strengthen' it?

Unfortunately, today we tend to polarized and absolutist thinking, believing that it must be one or the other. Even worse, social movements are generated that promote one option while cancelling or censoring the other, as if they were opposites. That is why in this book, and recognising that both are parts of a whole, we propose as a final objective to work simultaneously on both whenever possible. In this way we integrate both capacities, thus obtaining a useful and enjoyable 'stretching while strengthening'.

This can be done alternately (one time mobilizing and one time stabilizing) or simultaneously (actions requiring both capacities at the same time).

Integrative model

Analytical isolated
sectional model

Working on each capacity separately allows us to be more analytical and focus on that specific skill. This is effective for dissecting a part, but some actions are more difficult to transfer... For example, stretching a leg while sitting on the ground will not necessarily allow us to lift that same leg above our heads while standing... we need a complete scheme of mobility and stability. Insisting on one without the other can even affect the chances of achieving this.

By choosing movement patterns that include both aspects at the same time - stretching and strengthening - we will be closer to achieving holistic balance. Although these patterns may be more difficult to learn at first because they require multiple simultaneous capacities, their value lies in their practical applicability.

Can we start with isolated models? I mean, just stretching or just generating tension in our muscles in isolation? Yes, as I mentioned, these are analytical and reductionist models that allow us to understand specific aspects in isolation. However, it is vital to integrate them into complete models that have a direct transfer to the functions we wish to perform.

For example, I will not find it very useful to tense or stretch a muscle in my back in isolation while lying down, if I cannot then integrate that movement into a daily functional pattern, such as standing or walking. The key is to develop an understanding and training that connects these isolated exercises with functional, everyday movements, thus promoting a spine that is not only strong and flexible, but also functional and adapted to our needs.

Health is married with strength...

Historically, strength has had a very bad reputation. Strength is often confused with stiffness, contracture or clumsiness. This is a serious misconception that has existed from the first day someone trained with a load to the present day. It is even thought that strength can make our muscles slower and stiffer when in fact it provides more irrigation and nutrient exchange to our muscle cells.

If we think about it for a moment, practically EVERYTHING we do involves some kind of force, because we are living on planet Earth and we must manage our bodies in relation to gravity.

Personally, I achieved the best levels of connection with my body and reduced potential for injury when I 'friended' strength, when I found a balance between strength and other physical capabilities. I also recorded that muscle contractures and discomfort were reduced as I achieved a better balance of tensions and improved circulation in my structures.

Involving strength in your life doesn't mean you have to run out and lift heavy iron bars. Strength can be trained with weights that may look light or moderate but that you find challenging to manipulate. Even "strength" can be yoga poses, or performing weight shifts in a tai chi sequence. However, the reality is that the best stimulus your muscle cell will receive is when you train with some type of external load. Integrating this type of training into your routine can make a significant difference in your physical development, improving not only strength but also the body's functionality and endurance.

Health cannot be divorced from the strengh...

George Hackenschmidt encouraged strength work for health in his book "The Way to Live" over 100 years ago.

You can start by using everyday loads:
books, bags, purses, bags, packages...
anything will be fine if the load feels slightly
challenging but not dangerous.

The idea is to do it in a safe and controlled manner. Little by little you can mature from feeling like you are doing a casual physical activity to engaging in more serious training. We will call it "training" because it will be PLANNED and orderly. The moment you stick to a plan and are consistent with it, you are PLANNING, which is why we differentiate the simple physical activity of carrying grocery bags with training, as the latter is a physical activity that is planned.

2

Recognizing your spine

You don't need advanced knowledge or a magnetic resonator to recognize, claim and appropriate a structure that is yours in its own right: your spine.

Palpation and visualization are powerful tools to understand and locate this structure in your body.

You can use them in different orders according to your preference or even combine them. You can start by assimilating the information introspectively (reading and memorizing) and then apply it to the body (touching and visualizing) or vice versa.

There is no fixed rule, as each person will experience and learn differently.

The global spine

Your spine runs from your skull to your pelvis and is segmented into five parts: cervical, dorsal, lumbar, sacral and coccygeal. You will notice that the change between each zone occurs when the curves change from a convexity (bulge) to a concavity (dip), and vice versa. Some segments, such as the dorsal zone, are longer in length, while others, such as the lumbar zone, are shorter but larger. In addition, some segments have little movement in certain directions, while others allow a wide range of motion in all directions.

Global recognition

Manually accessing your own spine can be very easy or hellishly inaccessible, depending on the mobility of your shoulders. Therefore, you can opt for:

- Try to reach with your hands all the segments of the spine. This indicates a total autonomy of your upper limbs, which is very advantageous. If you barely reach and with a lot of effort, I recommend you take it easy to avoid annoying shoulder contractures.

- Reach only some parts of your spine and use, for example, an extending object, the floor, the wall or a ball. Through contact with an external element, you can feel those inaccessible segments.

- Ask another person to feel the different segments while you feel them.

Being able to reach all segments of your spine by yourself is very important because it reflects the autonomy you have over your own body. You can take this guideline as a measure of your improvements. Grooming, caring or the simple act of being able to scratch on your own are actions that we may not value when we can do them, but that we deeply regret when they are lost.

The curves

The segments of the spine are delimited by the change of curves, i.e. when a concave curve becomes convex. For example, this occurs in the change from cervical to dorsal spine. To understand this, we must be clear about the concept of concavity and convexity. Concavity can be understood as a 'cavity' or hollowing out or the inner area of a sphere. While convexity can be understood as a protrusion or the outer zone of a sphere. So, when we read that 'the dorsal spine has a posterior convexity', this describes that it forms a backward 'hump'.

Concavity is also described as lordosis.
Convexity is called kyphosis.

The curves are the mechanism by which the spine adapted to the relentless forces of gravity when humans began to walk on two feet. These curves act as a large spring-like shock absorber, counteracting the gravitational force. Therefore, the fewer curves the spine has, the less able it is to fulfil this function. The lack, exaggeration or inversion of any of these curves could lead to dysfunction, which can be aggravated by exercise, and even more so under the pressure of a load.

Convex

Concave

Recognizing the curves

A good way to recognise these curves is to lie down with your back flat on the floor, on a comfortable surface.

While lying down, without judging your position and structure, try to feel how many of your curves are in contact with the ground. The convexities, which are likely to be most noticeable in the sacral, dorsal and occipital (skull) areas, will be the ones you feel in contact with the ground. The concavities, such as the lumbar and cervical areas, will probably feel more separated from the ground. You can change these relationships slowly and with very small movements. For greater comfort, you can rest your feet with your knees bent and generate the movements from the roll of the pelvis, even noticing how the place of contact of the head changes.

By doing this, you will not only be recognizing the length
and shape of your curves, but also,
before you know it, you'll already be practising with your spine.
when mobilizing it during the reconnaissance process!

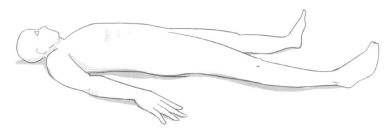

Visualizing the globality and activating the curves

Flexion in the lumbar region decreases the characteristic concavity of this area, and may even transform it into convexity.

Extension in the lumbar region increases the concavity (this term is known as lordosis). Thus, when we extend the lumbar region, we speak of an increase in lordosis.

Try to appropriate these movements to each area of your spine, always within a range of movement that is pleasant and free of pain or unusual sensations. You will find that there are areas where it is easier to extend, others where it is easier to bend, and others where these two movements meet in a balanced way. This is normal; not all areas have to be the same.

Perform all movements WITHOUT THE PRESENCE OF PAIN and without the intention of forcing a movement. For now, your attitude should not be to correct or to achieve more or less movement, but simply to recognise the zones and their possibilities.

Flexion increases
convexity

Extension
increases concavity

There are no right or wrong positions, only more or less convenient possibilities depending on the situation.

Global exercise for the curves

(Cat–Camel)

This will be our first mobility exercise, a classic taught in introductory levels, schools and bodywork academies. Although it may seem simple, don't underestimate its value: its main benefit lies in controlling the movement of the spine in a controlled and unloaded position.

This exercise works on the mobility of the entire spine, focusing on the relationship between the pelvis, head and lower back, as well as dorsal thoracic mobility. In addition, it offers an excellent cost/risk/benefit ratio, being a movement that practically everyone can perform without inconvenience.

As the name suggests, this exercise aims to increase and restore flexion and extension capacity
throughout the spine.

Start in the quadruped position, with your knees positioned directly under your hips and your hands firmly on the
floor. Make sure your elbows and wrists are in line with your
shoulders, forming a right angle (90 degrees) to the floor.

From this position, inhale as you extend your spine. Keep
your shoulder blades depressed (keeping your shoulders
away from your ears) and try to push your chest forward. At
the same time, perform a anterior pelvic tilt, bringing the
ischia towards the ceiling (pulling the tail out). The chin may
point slightly upwards.

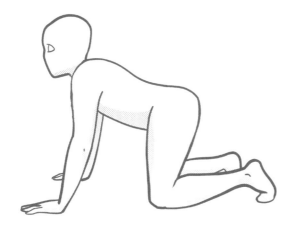

Exhale as you bend your spine. Seek to 'round' the back towards convexity, bringing the shoulder blades towards protraction (away from the spine). At the same time, move the pelvis towards posterior tilt, trying to make the coccyx point towards the floor. The neck should remain relaxed, the gaze directed towards the navel, but without bending the cervical area excessively.

Variation: As you gain mobility and experience in this movement, try starting the extension or flexion from one end of the spine. For example, start by extending the lumbar region and continue the movement progressively until you reach the cervical region. Then do it in reverse.

MOBILITY AND STRETCHING

We need to understand that being flexible does not necessarily go hand in hand with being mobile. To understand this concept, let's first define these two terms:

Flexibility: This refers to the ability of a muscle or group of muscles to temporarily lengthen. Flexibility is generally measured by how far a muscle can stretch.

Mobility: The ability of a joint to move freely and without restriction through its full range of motion. This will depend not only on flexibility but also on the health of the joint and the ability to stabilize the joint through muscle activity.

Thus, we can understand that a person can be flexible but not necessarily have good mobility. While flexibility focuses on the muscles, mobility addresses the overall movement of the joints and connective tissues.

Dorsal rotations in quadruped position

This exercise will help us to increase the mobility and rotational capacity of the dorsal spine:

1. Adopt the quadruped position, with your knees under your hips and forearms resting on the floor, elbows just under your shoulders and spine in a neutral position. From there, bring the tail towards the heels to reduce the involvement of the lower back. Then place one hand on the back of your neck. Do not pull down or put pressure on the neck with your hand.

2. From this position, bring the elbow of the arm resting on the back of the neck towards the opposite knee.

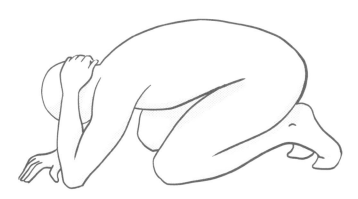

3. Exhale while flexing the spine. Try to round the back towards the convexity, bringing the shoulder blades towards the protraction (separating them). Keep the neck relaxed, with the gaze directed towards the navel.

4. From this position, bring the elbow of the arm resting on the head towards the ceiling. To do this, gently rotate from the dorsal area in the opposite direction to the previous movement. The aim is to reach a position in which the elbow and shoulder of the supporting arm are in line with the shoulder and elbow of the arm resting on the back of the neck.

The sets and reps will depend on your condition/situation but an average of 3 sets of 10 reps will be a good target. You can of course start with fewer sets and/or reps.

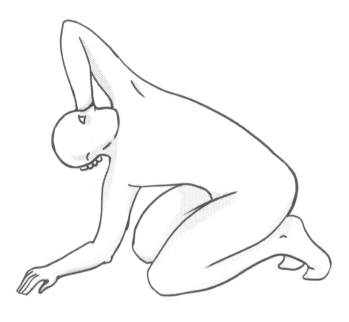

Holding things while standing

A first approach to strength training could be to introduce external resistance, such as loads or weights, into our system, or to try to support our own body by taking advantage of the resistance offered by our own weight. Let's start with external loads, which are easy to understand and whose resistance is visible.

The weights can be objects specifically designed for this purpose, such as dumbbells, kettlebells, balls or weights, or any other object easy to hold such as a bag, a book or a stone.

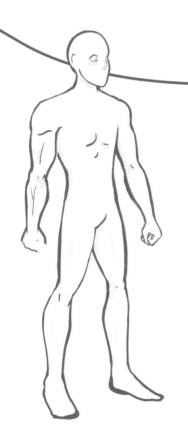

The amount of lifting you choose should be conditioned by your current capabilities.

It is important that you do not compare yourself with others, thinking that you 'lift too little' or that someone else 'lifts too much'.

What is considered 'a little' or 'a lot' depends on your own possibilities to interact with external forces and the current state of your body.

To start, you can hold an object in front of you. The difficulty of the exercise will depend on the load you choose and, very importantly, on how close (easier) or far away (harder) you position the load in relation to your body. As the seconds pass, you may notice that the muscles at the back of your trunk become active and begin to fatigue. This is a good sign; it means you are training those muscles to support you better.

Then try holding something behind you to feel the front wall of your trunk become more active.

Next, hold something on your sides and you will probably notice how the opposite side of the side you are holding becomes more active.

In the beginning, don't worry about counting sets or repetitions. Just do it as long as you can maintain correct technique and without any pain, discomfort or fatigue that will impair your ability to perform later.

IS IT MANDATORY TO PERFORM CERTAIN EXERCISES?

The simple answer is: it depends... At least in this book's approach, we try not to rely on absolutes but on relative ones.
By relying on absolutes, we don't take into account people's individuality and context.
By basing ourselves on relative, we are more concerned with what specifically THAT person needs. Therefore, even the exercises proposed in this book are SUGGESTIONS that can inspire us in the search for or development of other exercises.

Decompressing

An effective method for decompressing the spine, i.e. to generate tension by stretching and tending to separate one vertebra from another, is simply to hang on to something. Nowadays this recommendation has become so popular that you can even find it dosed by time, just like other recommendations such as walking a certain number of steps per day, sleeping a certain number of hours or drinking a certain volume of water.

You can do this on any firm surface that you can hang from, holding on with your hands and keeping your elbows fully extended. If you find it difficult at first due to lack of strength or a weak grip on your hands, you can start by hanging on an inclined plane. Although it won't provide the greatest stimulus to put longitudinal tension on your spine, it will serve as a useful progression to improve your grip.

You can also hang from a firm surface while supporting yourself with your feet or knees on the floor, or even sitting, thus reducing the load on your own body in the exercise.

Once you are able to hang with your body fully extended, supporting yourself only with your hands, allow the weight of your body to gently and naturally stretch your entire back.

And that's all there is to it! The hardest part will be maintaining the habit, just as it is with walking, bathing or drinking water.

You will find that many people use straps, inflatable devices or ropes attached to the skull and neck to generate a separating force in these areas. These manoeuvres, based on manual therapies, aim to achieve the same 'decompressive' effect as hanging but specific to the spine. Some apply it slowly and steadily, others quickly and even violently.

Although there is currently no clear evidence that demonstrates their direct effects on certain ailments or conditions of the cervical spine, if you try these methods and feel that they improve the situation of your vertebrae after these interventions, always do so with the caution, care and approval of a competent professional, previously ruling out any type of pathology that could put your health at risk.

Where is the cause?

One of the problems in dealing with any movement restriction and/or ailment is to focus excessively on a specific point on the body or on a specific pain. While a restriction or pain may manifest itself in one spot, it is part of the whole body system. Often, a dysfunction is only the small visible tip of an iceberg, but does not represent the whole iceberg. Similarly, pain may be an audible alarm that sounds in a specific area of a house, but does not necessarily indicate the cause of the pain. Remember, the cat is meowing through its mouth, but it has been stomped on its tail.

We remain terrified and watch for the alarm on the screen and not for the burglar entering from the other side. In the same way that leaks are evident when water runs down the wall, but the real cause is in the ceiling.

General daily recommendations

The causes of pain or dysfunction are multifactorial, so the better we control and optimise the factors that surround us, the more likely we are to avoid unfavourable situations. Do not underestimate the importance of the environment and the context in which you move day to day, paying attention and care to aspects such as:

Avoid sitting for prolonged periods of time.
If you have no other choice, try to intersperse it with periods of activity, doing small actions such as walking, climbing stairs or doing household chores that involve carrying, carrying or lifting.

Minimise impacts when sitting or lying down.
Control your descent so as not to hit the surface you are sitting on sharply.

Find an optimal personal sleeping position.
There is not ONE ideal position for the world's 8 billion people. It can be on your back, on your side or on your stomach. You may need to use cushions to accommodate different parts of your body.

Perform your body's daily tasks consciously and unhurriedly, giving you time for physiological needs such as eating and bowel movements. All of these processes require optimal time to tense, relax, breathe and move through them properly.

Nutrition, rest and stress reduction are key pillars which often amplify an ailment or dysfunction. Do not underestimate them, for it is difficult to find harmony if any one of these three elements is out of balance. Moreover, all three are within reach of modification on your own initiative.

As always, recommendations are not mandatory.
They are 'recommendations'.
You may need to develop your own recommendations
that are adapted to your situation and/or context and
write your own book!

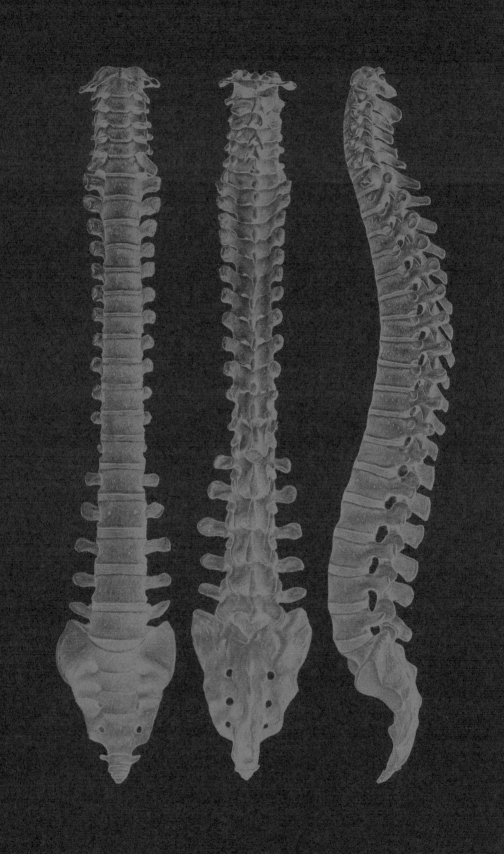

History of the spine: evolution and problems

3

The human body is often described as a 'perfect machine' or a 'masterpiece of engineering'.

However, when it comes to our spine, its design is not the most suitable due to the upright posture in which we find ourselves most of the time, fighting against gravity.

This situation reflects the result of an evolutionary process spanning millions of years, during which we have moved from a largely horizontal to a vertical stance.

This transition has come at a cost: the curves of our spine, which adapted to support verticality and gravity, can be a source of problems and pain. But this adaptation also brought with it significant advantages: verticality freed our upper limbs, which facilitated the development of more complex manual skills. This, in turn, boosted the evolution of our brains, expanding our cognitive and creative capacity.

Although the structure of our spine may not be 'bulletproof', it has been a key factor in the development of unique characteristics that define us as a human species.

The transition to standing upright has been costly

The conquest of the planet by humans, thanks in part to the cognitive development favoured by the bipedal posture, has come at a significant cost to our physical structure. We can find a list of 'disadvantages' associated with this evolution:

Increased pressure on the lumbar vertebrae: Gravity puts more pressure on the lower spine in the standing position, increasing the potential risk of injuries and disorders.

Additional bends in the spine: Adaptation to the upright posture has generated curvatures such as lordosis and kyphosis, the imbalance and exaggeration of which could cause postural and structural problems.

Compression of the intervertebral discs: This posture increases the compression on these discs, facilitating their potential premature wear and tear and conditions such as disc degeneration..

Stress in the cervical region: Holding the head on an upright spine increases the strain on the neck, increasing the likelihood of pain and stiffness.

Vulnerability to impact injuries: The bipedal position increases the risk of spinal injuries due to falls or impacts..

Increased pressure on the circulatory system: This posture increases pressure on the lower limbs, which can cause varicose veins and venous insufficiency.

Change in the arrangement of internal organs: The upright posture has altered the arrangement and support of the internal organs, which are now "stacked" vertically.

These disadvantages highlight how the transition to standing, while beneficial for cognitive development, has posed significant physical health challenges, especially exacerbated by contemporary sedentary lifestyles,

In addition, they warn us about the importance of not neglecting aspects such as decompression of the spine in different planes, efficiency in stability, active circulation and the ability to fall, roll and adapt to different terrains.

Your cervical spine

The cervical spine lies between the dorsal spine and the first bone of the skull (the occipital bone). It is composed of seven vertebrae that allow the head to be positioned in virtually any direction, while providing effective support for the skull. The cervical vertebrae are more circular in shape and are the smallest compared to the other regions of the spine.

The first and second cervical vertebrae have unique and particular shapes. The first cervical vertebra, known as C1 or Atlas, and the second, known as C2 or Axis, have a special design that facilitates head movement.

The cervical vertebrae are in close interaction with arteries, veins and nerves leading to and from the brain and spinal cord. This relationship is essential for blood flow to the brain and for the transmission of nerve signals through the neck to the rest of the body.

Cervical recognition

The cervical spine has a distinct concavity and this shape is easily palpable from behind. In the nape of the neck, the second cervical vertebra (axis) is the most prominent process below the skull, as the tubercle of the atlas (first cervical vertebra) is deeper and less prominent. The atlas can be felt, albeit with some discomfort or pain, in the space between the angle of the jaw and the mastoid process (the bony protuberance behind the ear).

The seventh cervical vertebra is very prominent and is often confused with the first dorsal. One way to differentiate the two is to note that the seventh cervical has less movement than the sixth cervical but more movement than the first dorsal. On palpation, these movements can be discriminated by flexion and extension of the head.

Your dorsal spine

The dorsal spine, located between the lumbar and cervical spine, is the longest segment of the spine, consisting of twelve vertebrae. These vertebrae are heart-shaped and intermediate in size between the lumbar and cervical vertebrae. A distinctive feature is that their spinous processes are longer and sloping downwards, which at some levels causes them to lie almost two vertebral levels below their respective bodies.

Because of their connection to the ribs and their function of protecting the organs within the rib cage, the dorsal vertebrae have relatively limited mobility. However, thanks to the number of vertebrae that make up this section, the total range of motion in the dorsal spine is significant.

Back recognition

Broadly speaking, the dorsal spine extends from the base of the neck to what is commonly known as the 'shoulder girdle'. Normally, this part of the spine has a noticeable convex shape, which in some cases may be exaggerated, forming a hump.

The spinous processes are a reference point, although it should be noted that in the dorsal vertebrae, their position varies. From the first to the fourth dorsal vertebra, the tip of the spinous process is at the level of its respective vertebral body. From the fifth to the ninth vertebra, the spinous processes are located at the level of one or even two vertebrae below. In the tenth to twelfth vertebrae, the spinous processes gradually come back into alignment with the level of their respective vertebral bodies.

The ribs can also serve as a guide to locate the dorsal vertebrae. From the second to the tenth rib, these are inserted between two vertebral bodies. For example, if we follow the path of the fourth rib, we will end up approximately between the bodies of the third and fourth dorsal vertebrae.

Your lumbar spine

We have already defined the spine as consisting of five parts: cervical, dorsal, lumbar, sacral and coccygeal.

The lumbar spine is situated between the dorsal spine and the sacrum and is made up of five vertebrae. These vertebrae are characteristically kidney-shaped, i.e. they are oval and resemble the shape of a kidney. They are quite large in comparison to the other vertebrae of the spine, which is essential for carrying most of the weight of the trunk.

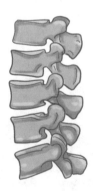

Lumbar examination

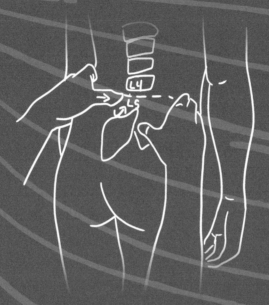

As a guide, you can draw an imaginary line that continues along your iliac crests. At about the height of these ridges is usually the fourth lumbar vertebra. From this point, you can count down to identify the fifth vertebra and up for the first three vertebrae. Remember that this reference may change from person to person, sometimes going as far as the third or fifth vertebrae. This process can be done on yourself or on another person. The most recognisable and palpable structure in this area is the spinous process, which is felt as a sharp protrusion at skin level. Although it is perceived as a beak, its shape is rather rectangular compared to the processes in other regions of the spine. In the lumbar region, this spinous process is at the same height as the body of the vertebra itself, which allows you to feel and know that most of the vertebra lies in front of this prominence.

Your sacrum and coccyx

The sacrum is located at the end of the spine, below the lumbar spine. It is connected above to the fifth lumbar vertebra and below to the coccyx. The sacrum is the fusion of five vertebrae, the shapes of which can still be distinguished within the bone. Its triangular shape allows the weight of the spine to be distributed towards the iliac bones and the lower limbs, fitting like a wedge between them.

The coccyx, colloquially known as the 'tailbone', is the terminal part of the spine. It is formed by the fusion of four to five vertebrae, which are almost unrecognizable due to their integration. Although often considered a remnant of our evolution, the coccyx plays an important role as an anchor point for several muscles of the pelvic base.

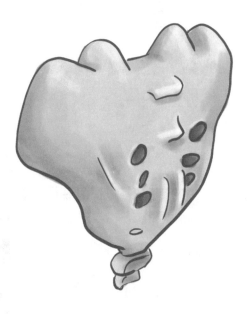

Sacral recognition

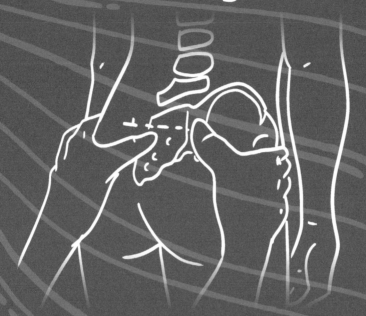

The sacrum is located at the end of the lumbar vertebrae, in the area where the direction of the curves of the spine changes from lumbar concavity to convexity at the sacrum. You can start counting the lumbar vertebrae from the fourth vertebra, which coincides with the iliac crest, until reaching the sacrum. In addition, the iliac crests can be palpated and their arcuate trajectory followed to the posterosuperior iliac spines, two bony prominences as the crests approach the sacrum, at the approximate location of the first fused sacral vertebra.

The coccyx is at the end of the spine, located in the intergluteal fold. Its palpation is simple, as it is the bony end portion and is followed by soft tissue near the anal area. When pressing the coccyx, it may present a micromotion, but it could also be uncomfortable because it is a very sensitive area.

Global cervical, lumbar, dorsal, and sacral visualization

Whether lying down, sitting, standing or moving, we can perform mental tours through all the structures we have described. This tour can be as an imaginary line that we draw with our mind or as a realistic 3D view of our structures. Either type of vision is valid as long as it allows us to approach a mental map of these structures.

In any position in which we are comfortable, either on our own body or on another person, we can make a global palpatory recognition. Thus, from the skull to the sacrum, we can recognize the basic curves and the changes between them, from convex to concave and vice versa.

We can also observe people in the street or pictures on the internet with their backs turned, and try, with the references we have given, to recognize first global areas and then even more specific vertebrae. This practice helps us to improve our understanding and recognition of the anatomy of the spine.

It is essential to establish and
reinforce a contact, either
by palpation, sensation,
imagination or visualization,
with the bony structures of
the spine.

We need to reconnect
the mind with the
physical structure!

A column of pearls

(Imagination and relaxation exercise)

We will imagine that our column is a transparent plastic tube and that in our head and neck we have accumulated a large number of balls, similar to large pearls. The pearls will begin to fall slowly through the tube-spine and will trace and mark an increasingly straight path. Our head and neck will feel lighter and lighter and with more freedom of movement. The pearls will not only trace the new straight path in the spine, but they will also sweep away any kind of discomfort or imperfection that comes their way.

Pack of 10 exercises to activate and stimulate the autonomy of the spine

This set of 10 exercises is versatile, evolving and can be adapted to various routines and environments. You can perform them all together, as a complete set, or break them up throughout the day into shorter sessions. I personally use them when I'm traveling, such as in airports or hotels, performing them in a grouped fashion. But I also incorporate them into my daily routine as a way of separating 30-minute blocks of work with each individual exercise, thus combining work productivity with movement and body activation. This way of integrating and presenting the exercises is just a suggestion. I encourage you to find the model that best suits your lifestyle and how you go about your day to day life.

Activating the system

When starting an organized workout, an excellent approach is to select a series of exercises that activate the circulatory system. This simple series of exercises is designed to 'pump' blood in three different areas of the body, activating and mobilizing from a specific segment to the entire system. The possible sensation experienced with these exercises will be primarily one of 'vascular activation' and mobility. Upon completion, you are likely to feel not only an activation of circulation and mobility in the area worked, but also in the spine and the rest of the body. Interpreting the spine as part of a whole integral system.

"TENSION" IS NOT A BAD WORD!

The word and even the concept of "tension" has been demonized in many body training circles for decades.

To demystify this conceptual error, it is essential to differentiate the terminology and note the effect that this word will have on the body. Tension refers to the state of partial or total contraction of muscle fibers during exercise, which is essential to produce movement and resist external forces.

However, this tension should not be a constant or chronic state. The presence of muscular tension during exercise is necessary to fulfill certain intra-exercise mechanisms and objectives, but it should not necessarily persist after exercise. In fact, an efficiently dosed and managed intra-exercise tension facilitates relaxation, circulation and optimizes physiological values after exercise.

Tension is not synonymous with stiffness or permanent contracture.

1. Shake arms backwards

Standing, we will perform an exercise where we will shake our arms backwards cyclically. Start with your hands at shoulder level and let them fall gently down and back, accelerating the movement towards the end of the stroke until you feel the fingers loosen. This gesture is a slightly exaggerated imitation of the natural swinging of the arms when walking but in a bilateral manner. Within your comfort level, you may choose to do extended sets of 100, 200, 500 or even more than a thousand repetitions, always taking care not to exaggerate the movement and to make it comfortable for the position of the shoulders. This exercise helps to activate circulation and relax the muscles of the arms and shoulders.

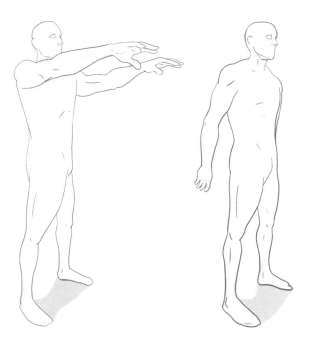

2. Leg pumping

With your feet apart at a comfortable distance that allows you to maintain your balance, perform the following exercise: first, stand on your toes, raising your heels off the ground, and then reverse the movement by raising your toes to stand on your heels. The movement should be cyclical but unhurried, trying to achieve as much range of motion as possible in both actions. In each lift, look for constant stability, avoiding stumbling or falling. Perform sets of 50, 100 or 150 repetitions, counting each repetition as a combination of lifting on your toes and then on your heels.

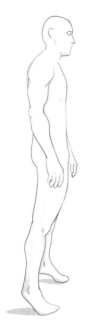

3. Central pumping

Standing, we will begin by expanding the abdominal wall as much as we can, as if we were 'pulling in the belly' as emphatically as possible. Then, we will do the opposite, contracting the abdominal wall as much as we can, as if we were 'pulling in our belly'. This movement will be like a continuous pumping between retraction and constant expansion, without hurry but without pause.

You can start this exercise on the floor, resting your hands on your abdomen or placing a book on it as a reference to better control the movement. It is important to perform this exercise as naturally as possible, without forcing any part of the body.

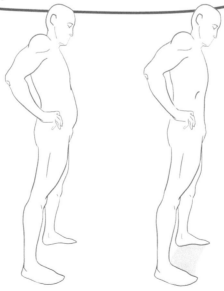

If you feel any discomfort, or if you have any specific condition such as a previous injury, obesity or pregnancy, and you have doubts about the effects of this exercise, it is advisable to consult a health professional before continuing.

3-dimensional fiber reorganization approach (Ba Duan Jing)

When approaching a muscle stretch, it is critical to understand that the first resistance is usually neural. This means that the muscle may offer resistance due to reflex activation of the nervous system that senses it has to avoid a potentially tissue-damaging position.

However, it is not only muscles that offer resistance. We also encounter fascia, tendons, skin and ligaments, many of these structures are composed of collagen fibers. Disorganization of these fibers can result in restricted movement. Therefore, we need to apply some type of force to align them in a more longitudinal and organized manner rather than parallel and disorganized.

In this context, an ancient sequence of Chinese tai chi and chi kung, known as the '8 pieces of brocade' (ba duan jing), offers a series of useful exercises to complete our series of 10 exercises (these will form from the 4th to the 9th).

Although the original sequence has eight exercises, for the sake of utility we will focus on the first six. For these exercises, we will establish:

• The proper placement to mobilize the parts of the body involved.

• The intention on the line of force we want to activate.

It is important to understand that these are global exercises for the trunk, so we will not seek to stretch a part of the body but a whole chain or ANATOMIC PATH of muscles (muscles chains). In this way, we will work on all the related structures and tissues that are arranged on our trunk, to activate and release the central structure which is the spine.

How should I breath?

Breathing is an adaptive process and can vary according to the function sought. To understand the how and when of breathing it is essential to understand how breathing works in relation to the body. To this end, two main approaches can be considered: physiological and mechanical.

Physiological approach: Respiration serves the function of satisfying the oxygen demands of the cells. If the cells need to generate more energy, a greater amount of oxygen is needed, which implies an increase in the frequency and/or depth of respiration. Conversely, if the cellular requirement is minimal, the respiratory system does not need to be activated as much.

Mechanical approach: The mechanics of breathing influences the internal pressures of the body. When inhaling, pressure is increased in the thoracic cavity (lungs) and in the abdominal cavity (due to compression of the diaphragm on the organs). This increased pressure can lead to greater stability in the trunk and increased tension in soft tissues such as muscles and fasciae.

With these two approaches in mind, there is no single "correct" way to breathe; rather, the way we breathe will depend on the desired function. This provides us with a powerful tool, as we can use both inhalation and exhalation as a strategy in our exercises. For example, we can use exhalation to reinforce relaxation and distension, and inhalation or apnea (air retention) to accentuate tension and increase stability over structures.

4. Holding the sky with your hands

Superficial and deep anterior muscle chain

HOW TO DO IT: Stand with your feet approximately shoulder-width apart and your hands together at pubic level. As you raise your hands, progressively raise your heels. Synchronize the movement so that, by the time your hands are above your head, your heels are completely raised and you are on your toes. The hands can be raised in a wide circle at the sides or directly in front of the body, ending with the fingers interlocked or one palm on the back of the other. What is really important is to apply tension on the front line of the body emphasizing the thrust of the hands.

EXECUTION: By pushing the ground with the feet and the 'sky' with the hands, two separating forces are generated that act by elongating the anterior structures and tissues of the trunk while activating the posterior structures by contraction and shortening. It is important that the exercise is active, generating two forces that try to divide or separate the body in two.

WHERE DOES IT ACT, WHERE WILL I FEEL IT?: Mainly on the central line of the trunk, from the chin to the pubis. This exercise not only acts on the muscular structures of the trunk, but also on the fasciae, ligaments and internal structures. The spine is 'stretched', generating an effect opposite to that produced by gravity, which tends to compress our spine in everyday life.

ADJUSTING: To add tension we will look to perform a really active push. As if you have a heavy load above you that you don't want to be crushed. You can also conserve air to get more tension by increasing internal pressure. Or exhale to help distend the structures in that position.

On the body we mark the superficial frontal anatomical pathway, where we will feel the application of tension by stretching.

5. Lateral bending

Lateral muscle chain

HOW TO DO IT: Stand with feet shoulder width apart (the closer together the feet are, the more demanding the movement). Raise one arm above your head. Keeping this arm extended, lean to the opposite side, passing the arm over your head. It is important not to bend or generate excessive load on the spine, but keep the trunk in the form of an arc. Instead of bending in isolation at an angle on a sector, try to make the extended upper hand, through an active push, try to reach a point as far away as possible, bending at the same time that you stretch in the form of an arc.

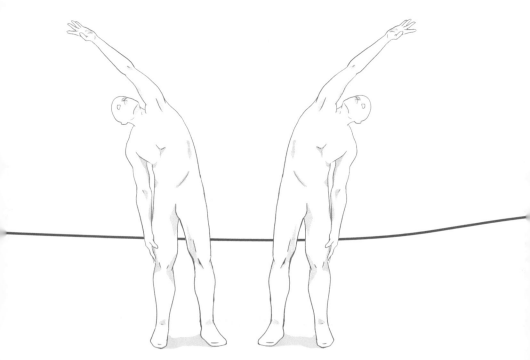

EXECUTION: This exercise requires keeping several forces active so that it is not completely passive. Here we will have a pushing force from the raised arm to the side and upwards, and another pushing force from the same foot as the raised arm, but in the opposite direction towards the floor.

WHERE DOES IT ACT, WHERE WILL I FEEL IT?: This exercise acts on the entire side of the trunk, and may extend along the arm and possibly to the side of the lower limb, even reaching the side of the ankles.

ADJUSTING: To add tension we will look for a really active push with the upper arm and in the opposite direction with the feet against the ground.

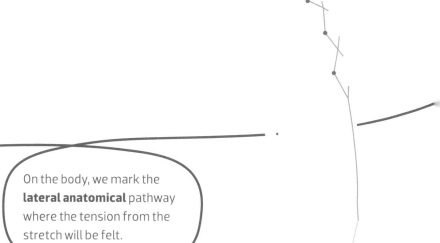

On the body, we mark the **lateral anatomical** pathway where the tension from the stretch will be felt.

6. The archer shoots an eagle

Anterior muscle chain, superficial and deep arm muscles chains

HOW TO DO IT: Standing comfortably, cross your hands. Next, extend one arm out to the side, keeping the wrist extended and the index finger as far out as possible. With the other hand, make an opposite movement, as if you were tensing a bow, closing your hand into a fist. This exercise can be done standing or in a 'horse' position (semi-flexed).

To vary the execution, change the hand position to a pronounced flexion of the wrist, and try pointing your index finger at yourself to add more tension on the structures of the back of the forearm and hand.

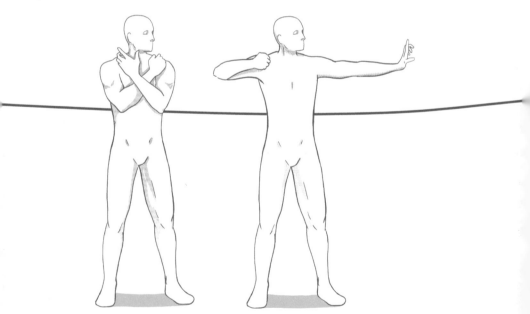

EXECUTION: The exercise requires simultaneous tensing in opposite directions. The extended arm should have the elbow and wrist as extended as possible. This tightness can be uncomfortable, but it is important not to run away from this sensation in order to correctly activates the structures.

WHERE DOES IT ACT, WHERE WILL I FEEL IT?: With the wrist in extension, you will feel the work mainly in the ventral region of the forearm, the inner arm and in the chest region. Variant: by changing the wrist to flexion, the activation will focus on the dorsal region of the forearm, arm and chest.

ADJUSTING: To increase tension, seek to create a similar and simultaneous force between the 'pushing' and 'pulling' arm. Between these two forces, the chest tissues will be in the middle and will be the most stressed.

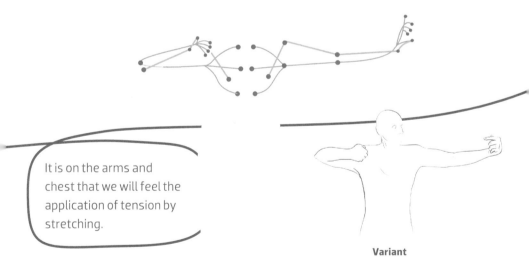

It is on the arms and chest that we will feel the application of tension by stretching.

Variant

7. Spreading the hands apart, on one foot

Spiral, cross and ipsilateral muscle chain (ipsi = same side)

HOW TO DO IT: This exercise has many variations, you can perform it with both feet on the floor, but an effective way to perform it is to combine it with balance training on one foot. Stand on one foot while raising the opposite knee. To increase the tension, raise the arm on the same side you are leaning on, creating a line of tension from the supporting foot to the hand extended overhead.

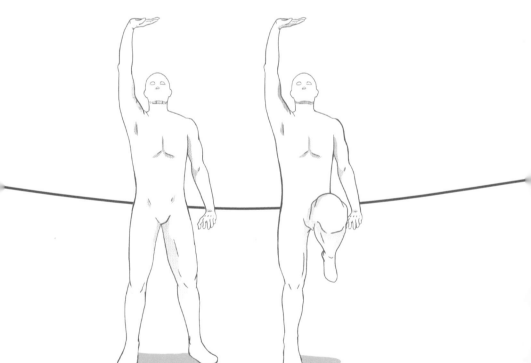

EXECUTION: The exercise consists of standing on one foot for as long as possible, which can vary from 10 seconds to 1 minute, depending on your condition.

WHERE DOES IT ACT, WHERE WILL I FEEL IT?: You will feel the activation all along the line you are setting up, from the supporting foot to the hand extended overhead on the same and opposite side depending on the configuration.

ADJUSTING: To add tension, perform an active push, as if you are holding a heavy load above you that you are trying to keep from crushing you. The elevated knee can be kept relaxed or you can try to push it as high as possible to increase tension.

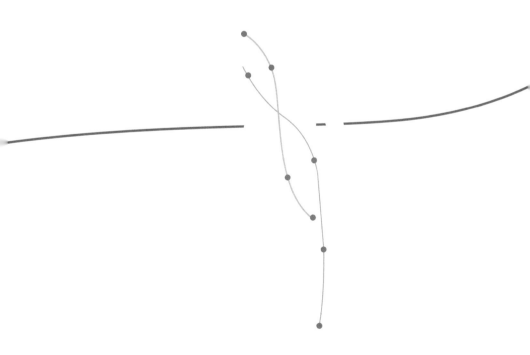

8. Rotations

Spiral muscle chain

HOW TO DO IT: Standing with your feet shoulder-width apart, point your toes slightly inward in a range that is challenging but comfortable. From this position, perform rotations to each side, moving primarily the trunk. The arms will accompany the movement, rotating the palms, which are initially facing your body, until finally facing outward. To increase the tension, extend the fingers of your hands to the maximum.

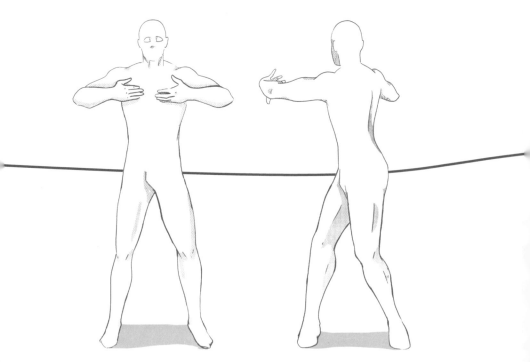

EXECUTION: This exercise involves a coordinated rotation of the body. The movement originates in the spine, but also involves shoulders, arms, hips, head, knees and foot segments.

WHERE DOES IT ACT, WHERE WILL I FEEL IT?: You will feel tension in the back of the neck, along a diagonal band across the trunk, and probably in the hips, legs, ankles and feet, especially if you keep the soles of your feet firmly supported.

ADJUSTING: To increase tension, emphasize the twisting by extending the fingers and pronating the forearms. The gaze can also intensify the movement, reaching as far as possible without causing discomfort.

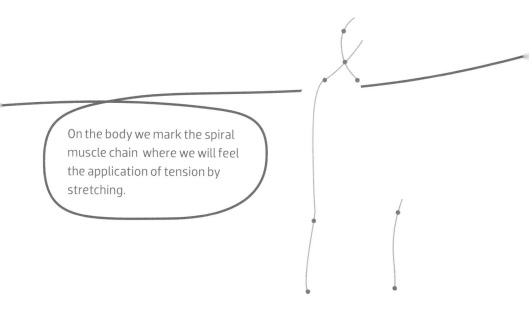

On the body we mark the spiral muscle chain where we will feel the application of tension by stretching.

9. Posterior chain

Posterior muscle chain

HOW TO DO IT: Standing, bend from the hips and spine in a proportionate manner. The hands should try to reach or go towards the floor, but reaching is not mandatory. The important thing is to feel how the entire posterior chain is activated through the stretch. From this position, you can stand up again to continue the exercise in a cyclical manner. If you prefer, you can coordinate the movements with your breathing, which can help you relax in the lower position and generate more tension on the way up.

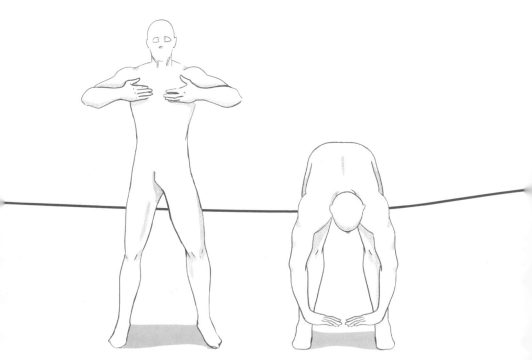

EXECUTION: This exercise involves folding in on yourself. Although it will be felt primarily in the back and posterior region of the legs, the posterior chain extends from the skull to the soles of the feet.

WHERE DOES IT ACT, WHERE WILL I FEEL IT?: You will feel a tightness from the back of your skull to your calves and feet. You may find some areas stiffer than others; this is not a problem, but indicates that you may have greater restrictions in different parts of the body.

CAUTIONS: Avoid this type of movement if you have sensitivity, discomfort or pain when bending the spine.

On the body we mark the posterior anatomical pathway, where we will feel the application of tension by stretching.

10. Spine wave

General spine

HOW TO DO IT: It begins with a general flexion of the entire spine. Comfortable and pleasant. From that position, start the extension starting with the sacrum, followed by the lumbar, dorsal, cervical and finally the skull, as if it were a progressive wave. It is important to perform this wave with an S shape and with as little effort as possible. You could also start from the skull or from the middle of the spine. The important thing is that once the wave is started, it is not interrupted.

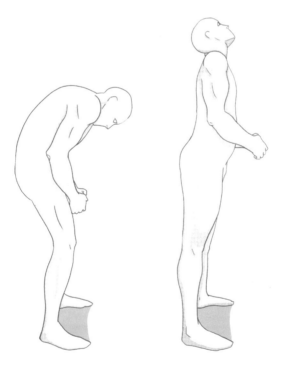

EXECUTION: This exercise involves all segments of the spine. The vertebrae and surrounding structures, including the intervertebral discs, receive compressive and separating stimuli in all sections.

WHERE DOES IT ACT, WHERE WILL I FEEL IT?: You should feel no pain or strange sensations. The movement is continuous, meandering and almost hypnotic. The sensation is one of increased freedom and movement in all sections of the spine and in its composition as a unit.

ADJUSTING: To add more planes of motion, to these combinations of push-ups and extensions you can add slight bending and rotating movements in all directions, as long as they are within a safe range and do not cause discomfort.

Clarifications and recommendations

An orthodox classicist might find that these 10 exercises are something different or that they deviate from a traditional training model (as in a Tai Chi or Chi Kung class). That thought is accurate, because in fact the exercises have been modified. Even the names have been changed for better understanding and memorization.

This 10 pack of exercises is a compilation that I have modified to fulfill a basic function: to promote freedom of movement of your trunk. This also gives us the guideline that each person can create their own exercise package to fulfill a personal function and objective. These 10 exercises make up my personal package, which I believe could be comprehensive for most people. In fact, at this very moment (February 15, 2024) I intersperse 30 minutes of writing this book with one or two of these exercises, so you can take this package as is, use only part of the sequence, or modify it to your liking.

Because of this, it is also important to pay attention not only to the exercises but to contemplate the underlying theory of this book, so that you can understand the form, function and possibilities of your spine. By understanding how things work, you will be able to establish a more personalized plan with the development or creation of others or your own exercises if needed.

Exercise sequences
should be adapted to
your personal needs and
objectives.

It is not productive to spend
years trying to adapt to an
exercise or system that
does not fit your specific
needs and requirements.

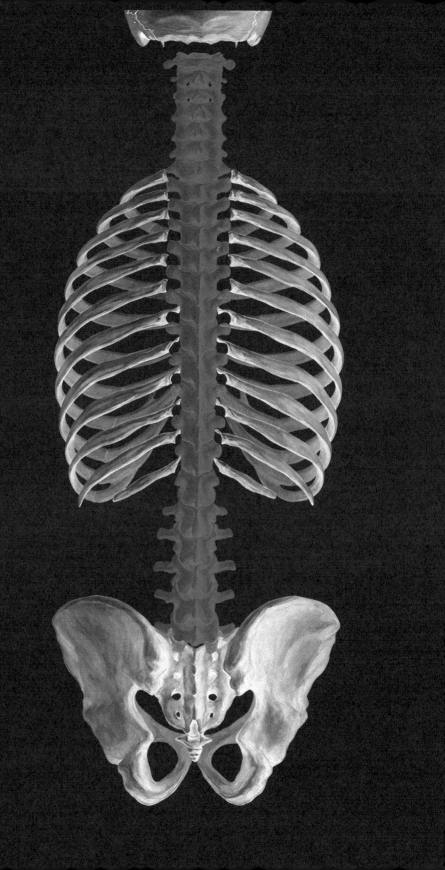

How much is too little and how much is too much?

4

We live governed by limits: how much is too little? how much is too much? when is it too much?

In the same way in the body we always face the problem of determining how much is too little or too much, reinforced because all bodies could be different.

When setting your spinal ranges of motion, we encounter a similar dilemma. How much is too little? How much is too much? What is advisable? Is the range the same for an office worker as for someone who was born in the Peking circus?

To discern this we will talk about GLOBAL AND ESTIMATIVE ranges of movement and always take into account the characteristics of the person and his context, to have an approximate idea of the possibilities of movement of his spine.

Estimated ranges of movement of the spine

Although there is no absolute consensus on the overall amplitude in a joint or group of joints, due to anatomical variants between individuals and different measurement sources, I present here an average of all measurements recorded in the following trunk areas. If you find it difficult to understand the angles, you can better guide yourself visually by estimating with the drawings.

LUMBAR RACHIS:

Flexion: 60° (52° a 59°). 8° to 20° per vertebral level.

Extention: 35° (15° a 37°).

Lateral tilt: 20° (14° a 26°). 3° to 6° per vertebral level.

Rotation: 5°. 1° a 2° per vertebral level.

Global flexion
of the entire spine: 140°

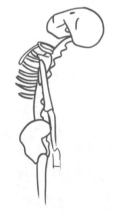

Global extension
of the entire spine: 140°

THORACIC RACHIS:

Flexion: 45°. 3° to 12° per vertebral level.

Extention: 40°.

Lateral tilt: 20° (high vertebrae 2° to 4°, low vertebrae 4° to 9°.).

CERVICAL RACHIS:

Flexion: 40°.

Extention: 60° to 70°.

Lateral titl: 35° to 45°.

Rotation: 60° to 80° (Atlas/Axis 40° according to the author).

At the moment, you don't need to worry about specific degrees, you need to get it out of your head that certain degrees are right or wrong. Instead, it is more important to have a visual idea about the common range of motion that the spine possesses and based on that work to approximate or maintain an approximate that is commensurate with your needs.

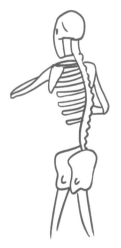

Global rotation: 120°

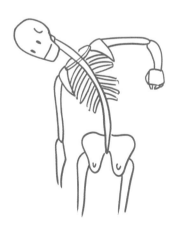

Global lateral tilt: 80°

Specific Structures: The atlas (C1)

When we speak of 'the atlas' or 'the axis', we refer to the specific names given to certain vertebrae. The atlas, in this context, corresponds to the first cervical vertebra, counted from top to bottom. It is also known as C1, where 'C' is the abbreviation for 'cervical' and '1' indicates that it is the first vertebra in this section.

The name 'atlas' comes from Greek mythology, in which Atlas holds up the entire world. Similarly, in the human body, the atlas supports your head.

This vertebra, the atlas, differs markedly from the others in that it does not have a vertebral 'body' (the cylindrical structure that we usually observe in the anterior part of the vertebrae). Therefore, its shape is more similar to that of a ring.

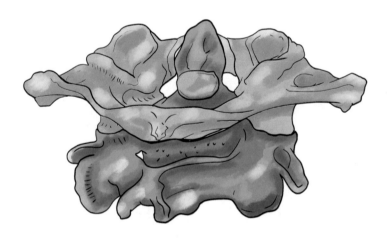

Understanding the atlas

The atlas, being a difficult vertebra to access, can be palpated carefully at the nape of the neck. Under the skull and above the spinous process of the second cervical vertebra, the posterior tubercle of the atlas can be barely felt in projection when palpating behind the nape of the neck. Moving the skull forward or backward can facilitate the sensation of projection of this tubercle through the tissues under your fingers.

Also with great caution, since it is an extremely sensitive area, you can palpate the transverse processes of the atlas, which are lateral bony prominences. These are located between the angle of the mandible and the mastoid process, which is behind the ear, between the muscle fibers. Rotating the skull to one side and to the other can make this prominence more or less obvious to the touch.

Specific structures: The axis (C2)

The axis is the second cervical vertebra, counted from top to bottom, so it is called C2 (C for cervical and 2 for second).

The name 'axis' is derived from the word 'axis', reflecting its function as the axis of the vertebra above it, the atlas. This axis is an extension of what was the former body of C1 and acts as an actual mechanical axis, allowing the vertebra above it, the atlas, to perform rotational movements, similar to making denial gestures with the head.

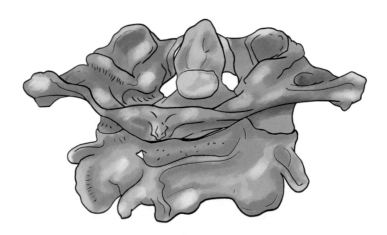

Understanding the axis

The spinous process of the axis (also known as the posterior tubercle) is easily palpable. On the surface, it is the first noticeable tubercle that can be palpated moving from the skull downward. Flexion and extension of the skull make this tubercle more or less prominent to the touch.

In the same way as with the atlas, we can also palpate laterally the transverse processes of the axis, although this implies separating some tissues. Sometimes this palpation can be uncomfortable or even painful due to the sensitivity of the area.

Once you locate these three structures of the axis, the posterior spinous process and the two lateral transverse processes, you can palpate all or some of them at the same time with one or two hands. This will allow you to hold the vertebra practically in your hands, giving you a tangible sense of its location and structure.

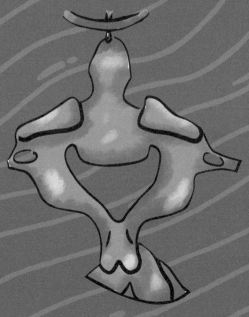

Specific structures: Seventh cervical (C7)

C7, or the seventh cervical vertebra, is the next vertebra we will analyze, since, like C1 and C2, it has distinctive characteristics compared to the other cervical vertebrae.

These special characteristics give it properties of both the cervical and dorsal spine. In addition, it is more voluminous relative to the other cervical vertebrae, and its spinous process is much larger and more distinct than the rest of the cervical vertebrae, making it particularly notable in the structure of the spine.

Knowing your seventh cervical vertebrae

When descending along the cervical spine, we will find a vertebra much more prominent than the others. Immediately below it, we will also find another prominent vertebra (D1 or first dorsal), which sometimes makes it difficult to differentiate them. By making contact with both, we can flex and extend the head and the cervical spine. In this movement, the vertebra that moves the most will be the seventh cervical vertebra, which has much more movement than the first dorsal vertebra, which is more limited.

The other cervical vertebrae

The rest of the cervical spine, consisting of the C3, C4, C5 and C6 vertebrae, generally has a small vertebral body and transverse processes with a foramen through which arteries and veins pass. This feature underlines the importance of keeping this area clear to ensure optimal cerebral irrigation. In general, these vertebrae have a high range of mobility in all directions.

To palpate these vertebrae, you can take as a reference the most easily palpable ones, C2 and C7. Try to discern and count the structures between them one by one. This group of four vertebrae is quite close together, which sometimes makes it difficult to recognise them individually.

Don't use pain as a parameter in training.

OUR QUEST IS FOR
AUTONOMY. THAT IS WHY
THE MOST USEFUL BENCHMARK
FOR US IS TO TRY TO OVERCOME
A RESTRICTION OF MOVEMENT OR
THE IMPOSSIBILITY OF STABILIZING
SOMETHING. TAKE THESE TWO
REFERENCES AS A GUIDELINE
FOR IMPROVEMENT.

Using pain as a reference generates a toxic bond with your body.

Basic neck mobility

The cervical area allows wide movements in all directions. The imperative need of our species to maintain visual control on all planes (just imagine having to survive in the jungle depending on the registration of your gaze in the face of predators) provides humans with extended movement possibilities in this region. We can maintain the possibilities of head and neck movement by increasing the daily inoculation of these gestures in a very simple way.

1. **Carry the head forward and down, and backward and downward.**
2. **Turn the head to the side.**
3. **To carry the head sideways by bending.**
4. **Rotate the head in complete circles.**

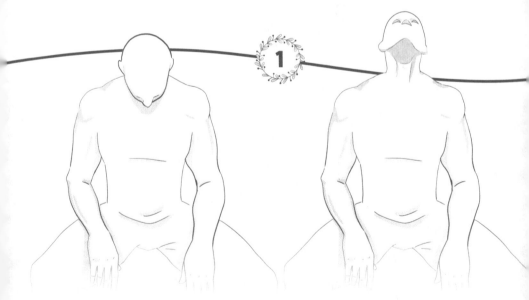

Cervical mobility exercises can be performed with a number of repetitions that you find comfortable and challenging, such as 5, 10 or 15 repetitions. It is important to consider the context in which these exercises are of most benefit to you, taking into account aspects such as the time of day, your personal situation and the place where you perform them. Always avoid pain and uncomfortable sensations. This sequence is simple but relentlessly logical and practical in maintaining autonomy and activity in this area.

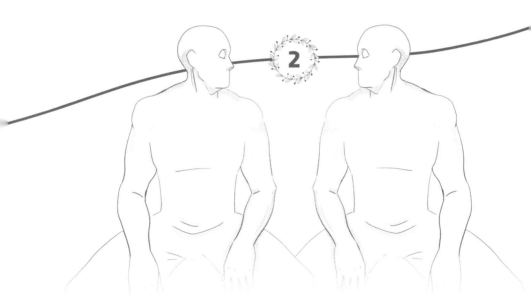

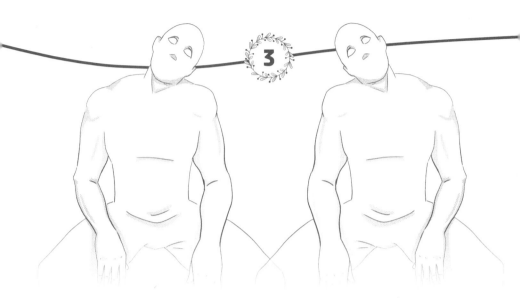

REMEMBER

The exercises mentioned above are aimed at recovering or maintaining the autonomy of the spine.

It is not about setting records or achieving rigid, arbitrarily imposed ranges of movement.

The important thing is just to compare yourself to yourself and record if the movement increases or if you feel that it takes less effort to do it. Don't go by measurements or ranges of movement that you see in a photo or that someone else has proclaimed as necessary to achieve.

Going slowly and without 'pulling' helps to improve mobility without pain.
The important thing is to feel improvement in your own body and to maintain the autonomy of your spine.

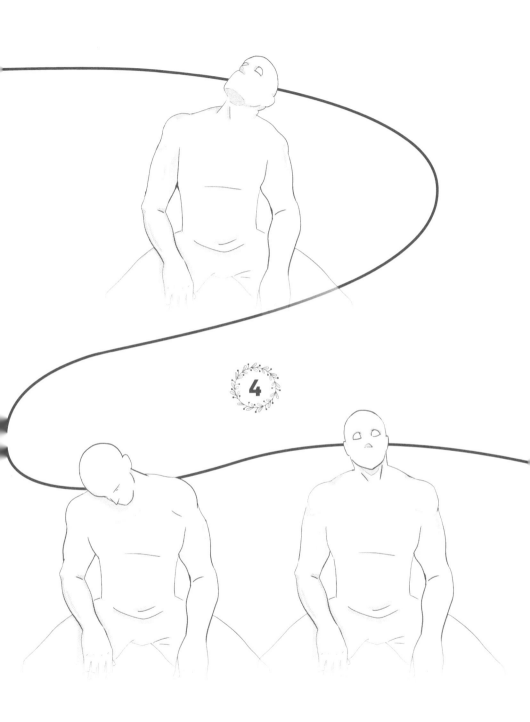

Visualizing the vertebrae

Using the descriptions and drawings of the vertebrae that we have presented, we can try to visualize them. The methods will be very personal and valid for each person, as we are all different, so here are some simple and varied visualization tips:

- Start with an easily recognizable and palpable part that you have already been able to touch, such as the spinous processes of a vertebra.

- From there, you can visually roam around using your imagination. Anything goes, it can be a perfect 3D image, an imaginary light running through the structures, or an imaginary pencil. Find the technique (whatever you can think of, however delusional it may seem) that you identify with best.

- Within this recognition, try to differentiate the right side of the structure from the left. Do you find one more difficult than the other? Is it more difficult to imagine or recognise one side? Do you feel that you visualise one side larger than the other?

- If in doubt, you can always revert to other resources such as discriminative palpation or help with real images of the structure.

Increasing stability

Specific core stabilization work, as a protective mechanism for the spine, has gained popularity in recent decades. However, for everyday activities such as standing and nullifying the effects of gravity, extensive work and/or preparation is not really needed. In my opinion, core work is valid but is often overdimensioned and can be overrated for the average person. Despite this, increased stability work can be useful for everyday tasks such as carrying, lifting, standing, holding something, or performing simple jobs with repetitive gestures. Specific stabilization in 'useful' postures can make these actions more efficient.

In addition, trunk stabilization is a prerequisite for activities or disciplines where external forces interact, such as martial arts, weightlifting or high intensity tasks. This stabilization is often achieved with specific training that has good transfer to these activities. However, sometimes training of the specific gestures of these disciplines may be sufficient to provide adequate stabilization.

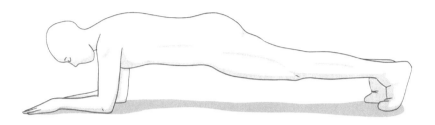

Although trunk stabilization work is essential for certain activities and sports, its importance can be relativised for activities of daily living and adapted according to individual needs and objectives.

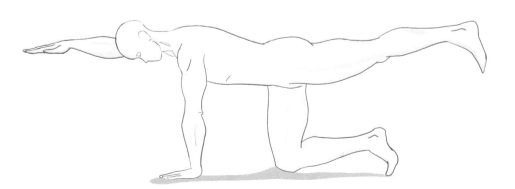

Standing planks

'Plank' training is a very simple concept. Like a plank that does not bend, the aim is to keep the body as straight as possible. This will force you to activate certain muscle groups responsible for holding the trunk in place. Thus, we get used to the fact that when an external force (such as gravity, a weight or a load) acts on our system, we resolve it by stabilizing its axis, our spine, with the help of specific muscles that prevent certain movements. We can start simply and with minimal effort: a standing plank supported against a wall. You can rest your elbows and hands on the wall, and the farther you position yourself from the support point, the greater the difficulty of the exercise.

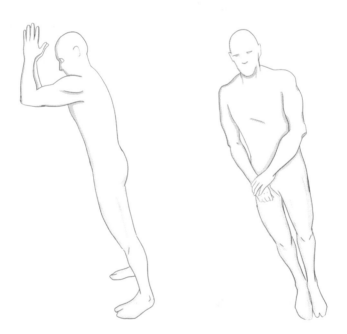

It is also a good progression parameter: if we can't stay leaning against the wall in a standing position and slightly inclined, we are probably not ready to perform a plank of greater difficulty, such as on the floor in a horizontal position.

Also, on a stable surface, we can look for some kind of lateral support to resist lateral tilting.

What we are looking for in these training models is to find uneven supports on stable surfaces, which require us to resist flexions, extensions, lateral tilts and rotations. This can be done, for example, with the structures we find in a square or park.

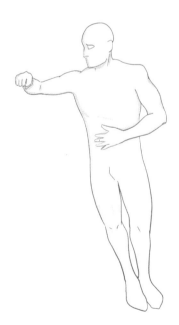

How long we should stay in each position depends on the individual. The best advice at the beginning is to achieve a good FORM and to have proper control over the avoidance of movement. With a little practice, we can change levels until, for example, our body is aligned with the horizontal of the floor.

Subsequently, we can establish arbitrary times in which we feel that the effort increases, either because of the difficulty of the plank or because of the time we spend on it. It should be noted that this time will not be the same for everyone. A good starting point might be to hold each posture for a minimum of 8 seconds and up to a maximum of 30 seconds for the average person.

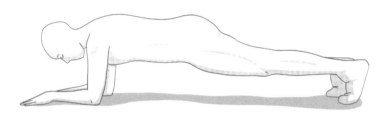

DOES THE CORE EXIST?

The concept and categorization of core is just a grouping of theories and a useful way of categorizing exercises with structures. It is a rather overdimensioned concept at present, and it is difficult to establish and support its concepts 100% with scientific evidence.

This does not detract from the fact that from an empirical approach you may find that increasing your trunk stabilization can help you in specific tasks. The reality is that for simple, everyday tasks, you need little stabilization of this type, but for carrying things or holding objects in a specific way, specific core training seems to help stabilize these structures.

Bird dog and asymmetric planks

A good approach to working on trunk stabilization are these two exercises that are considered 'safe' by general consensus among most coaches. In them, we distribute the effort between the lower and upper limbs, thus challenging the stabilization of the spine. The difficulty lies in the asymmetry, as we hold one lower limb while holding the opposite upper limb. Thus, we must avoid not only the flexion and extension of the spine, but also its rotations and lateral tilts. While these are good base exercises, remember that you are performing them in an unusual position for the body's normal daily functions.

In the bird dog, we rest on the ground on one knee and the opposite hand. We extend the free leg backwards to balance it and the free arm forwards, trying to stabilize for at least eight seconds. Then, alternate sides, always trying to maintain the neutrality of the spine.

Dead bug

In the deadbug we will work on a similar concept to the bird dog but while lying down. Here, we will try to avoid trunk extension. The idea is to achieve and stabilize a lower limb raise with a crossed upper limb raise. The aim is to maintain neutrality of the spine. To do this, we can start by progressing the exercise by lifting the lower limb with the knee bent, and over time progress to its final form. Remember that in these exercises, when you want to make them easier, you should bring the body parts closer to the center and when you want to make them more difficult, you should move them further away. In this way, you can adjust the difficulty of the exercise.

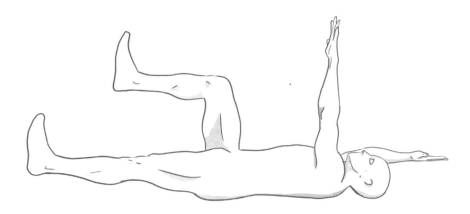

All the planks

A very generalized concept is that the planks must be straight figures. To begin with, we already know that our spine is not a straight board in its physiological position, but contains the curves we have already studied. But something that is seldom considered is the variety of positions that the spine offers: shouldn't we also be able to keep it stable in flexion, extension or inclination positions? To this end, we will seek to stabilize the spine in positions of flexion or extension, or rotation, but always bearing in mind that the forces or loads we impose on these schemes must be less than those we impose on the spine in a neutral position. It is also important to make sure that any force we introduce into our system in a position that is not straight, and which produces pain or a strange sensation, is carefully evaluated, as it may indicate that we are unable to perform it due to the particular situation of each person.

Getting up from the floor: strength + mobility

The reverse Turkish get-up is a fundamental exercise for functional autonomy. It allows strength to be applied from different positions, such as lying, kneeling or sitting, and during transitions between them.

This movement involves precise control of the spine to descend and rise from the ground in a controlled manner, while maintaining operative movements in the arms. This skill is essential for independence and functionality in daily life, especially as we age.

Imagine being over 60 years old and being able to get up from the floor without assistance, while maintaining freedom of movement in your arms. The reverse Turkish get-up aims to improve this ability, stimulating your autonomy and quality of life.

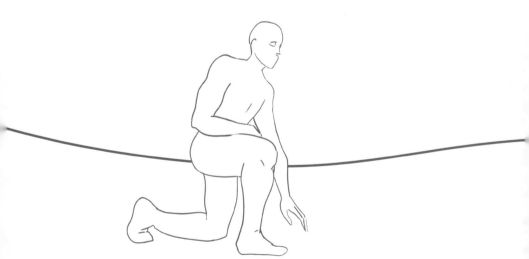

Before you start, I would try simply trying to go to the ground and then stand up in whatever way you can. This will allow you to make a basic assessment of what condition you are in.

The entire exercise begins standing (the entire reverse sequence on page 121), with one arm raised above the head, or we can begin without requiring any additional arm action. Then bring the foot opposite the raised arm backwards, resting it on the floor. The knee is then bent into a lunge position. Holding this position, support the hand opposite to the one that is raised (which will always be as vertical as possible above the head). Using this new support, try to pass the foot that was behind you under your body until it is in front of you, allowing you space to sit on the floor. Then try to lie down on the floor in a controlled manner. Once on the floor, we sit up in a natural way without necessarily respecting the reverse order of the exercise, helping ourselves with whatever is necessary. Then repeat the exercise on the other side.

Stand up from the floor with autonomy (classic Turkish get-up):

We will perform all the previous steps but adding the difficulty that we will be lying on the floor. Here, gravity and the weight of our body will be our greatest resistance, making this version more difficult for many.

Start on the floor with your arm above your head, vertical to the floor. From there, we will try to go to the sitting position, not directly, but first rotating a little to the side and then sitting up (don't worry, in the following pages you will find all the drawings). To do this, we can help ourselves by leaning sometimes on our elbows or hands. It is essential that the arm above the head is always as perpendicular as possible to the ground. From the seated position and with the help of the support of the foot of the limb that was flexed, and with the support of the hand that was behind, raise the hip sufficiently so that the foot of the extended limb can pass underneath us until the knee is supported. From there, we will move into a lunge position, which will make it easier for us to end up standing up completely.

Once we have trained the downstroke and the upstroke, we can combine them into a complete movement that we will call the 'classic Turkish get-up' or 'TGU'. When this movement is well controlled, we can perform it with weights: a small dumbbell, a few kilos package, or any comfortable and safe object to hold.

This all-round exercise not only improves stability and strength, but also promotes coordination and body awareness. Adding weight increases the challenge, leading to further development of these skills. However, it is important to ensure that the technique is correct before introducing any additional load.

GETTING OFF THE GROUND
HOW TO SELF-ASSESS?

Getting up from the floor is a simple and inexpensive evaluation proposal suggested by my friend and colleague Jerónimo Giraudi. It consists of asking the person to get up from the floor by his or her own means. This exercise provides an easy way to identify which elements, both structural and coordinative, present the greatest difficulty, allowing work to be done to improve them.

The act of getting up from the floor thus becomes a guideline, an evaluation test and an exercise in itself for the rest of one's life.

Leisure recommendations for your spine

A historical and hegemonic thought implanted in our minds is that there are 'right' and 'wrong' postures. This thinking has also extended to situations where we are supposed to be relaxed or thinking about other things, such as leisure, recreation or free time. Thus, we are bombarded daily with recommendations on how we should sit, lie down or stand when we are watching TV on the sofa or playing a video game on our computers or consoles. However, recent studies have shown that it is not the posture itself that is important, but the time we spend in that posture, with the effect of decreased circulation to an area being more serious than the possible structural effect. Your tissues are prepared to bear weight, to stretch, to contract (especially in an unloading position such as a sofa or chair), but not indefinitely.

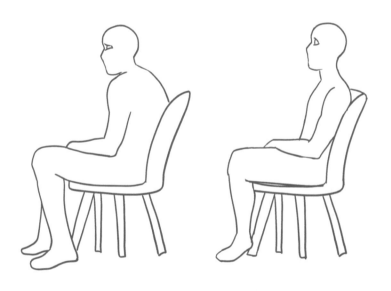

When you are sitting simply find a posture that is comfortable for you, without anatomical or ergonomic judgement or prejudice. But try to change every few minutes. Don't worry so much about the posture itself (as long as it doesn't cause pain or numbness), but about not staying in it for too long. Think of your system not as something structural, but as something circulatory...

When you are in intermediate positions between sitting and lying down, try to change position, either naturally or, if you are more organized and disciplined, every few specific minutes, moving from one specific posture to another (if necessary you can use a watch or an alarm for this purpose).

When standing, you can also alternate between a resting posture and a more active one, trying to distribute the weights in a balanced way, once to one side and once to the other. Remember, there is no universal posture; the important thing is that the system does not stagnate and that you can keep the circulation in your tissues active.

Loading things

There is a universe of recommendations on how to carry things at work and in everyday life, from our grandmothers' recommendations to "lift with your legs and not your back" to scientific studies and entire books on techniques for lifting things from the floor or from a table.

In order to take care of our back when lifting something, we have to take into account a concept that is rarely considered: the context and the situation of the person.

The context includes factors such as how much effort the load involves for the person, where the load is located, what shape it is in, and what physical/emotional state the person is in. Lifting a piece of paper in your home is not the same as trying to lift a heavy anvil in the middle of a ship that is sinking in a storm.

The context tells us whether we can lift it in any way we can think of or whether we need to prepare the body in a specific way. If the load does not involve great effort, skill or challenge, we can probably lift it with our back bent, as our spine is prepared to stabilize itself in any position with a low load.

The person's situation includes aspects such as fatigue, injuries, sensitivity to certain movements, insecurity or stress. In this situation, it does matter how the lifting is done, as even when lifting a paper from the ground the person could be injured if his or her situation conditions or determines the state of his or her structures. Therefore, there is no right or wrong way to lift; this will be determined by the context and the momentary situation of that person.

Basically, if you need to lift something that is below you, you can use your knees more effectively.

If the load is in front, you may have to use more movement from the hips, and if it is somewhere in between, perhaps both mechanics. However, if the weight is effortless and your personal situation is optimal, you may be able to lift it as you are most comfortable without necessarily affecting your structures.

If you need to know how to lift more specifically (at work or with specific machinery or apparatus), I recommend looking into literature that includes advanced concepts on specific training or ergonomics.

Farmer's walk

One of the simplest and most fundamental exercises, which works on carrying and carrying things, is the 'farmer's walk'. To perform it, you don't need specific implements, unless you're looking to lift a world record.

What we seek and achieve with this practice is to try to maintain structural integrity under load, which is paramount to our daily life on this planet as we constantly and unfailingly have to interact with external objects and forces.

As we have mentioned, modern thinking and the latest research questions to what extent and with what magnitude we have to train our trunk to avoid movements. But from a functional point of view, our trunk should be able to generate movement, avoid movement and, within the generation of movement, avoid other movements. This means that the trunk should not only be strong and stable, but also flexible and adaptable to different situations and loads.

In the farmer's walk, we simply carry a weight in one (called a bag) or both hands (called a farmer) and walk while maintaining an upright and stable posture. This exercise not only strengthens the trunk muscles, but also challenges our ability to maintain stability while moving. Moreover, as a functional exercise, it mirrors many of the everyday activities we perform, such as carrying things or moving objects at home or at work.

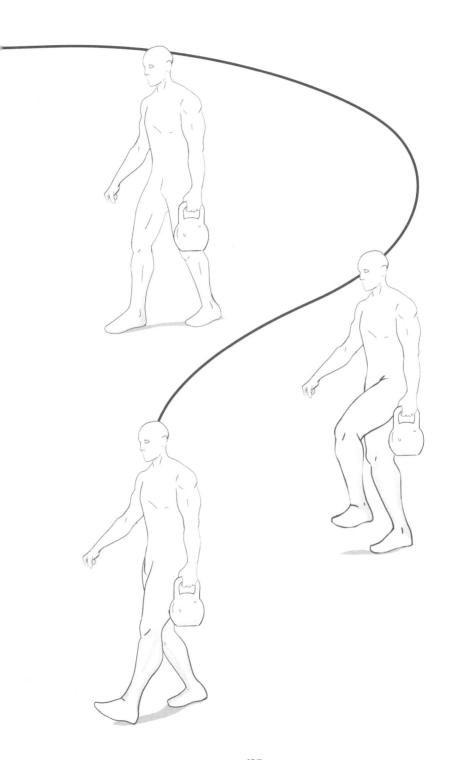

Starting transport from different positions

The basic starting position usually used for lifting weights is by carrying the object next to us, so that we resist sideways tilting at the start of the load and the transport. However, we can also start from different positions, as the weight will not always be at our sides. Sometimes we can start with the weight in front of us, perhaps a little diagonally, sometimes crossways (e.g. take something in our right hand when the object is on our left), and sometimes even with the weight behind us. The latter are the situations where we have to be especially careful about the amount of load, to make sure that it does not exceed our capabilities. Here we will be going for the weight in far away positions involving combined twisting or bending, so we will be much more careful in choosing the load and paying attention to stabilising our trunk.

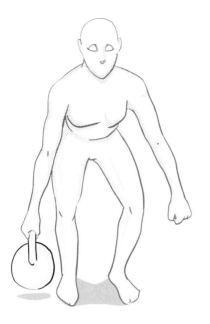
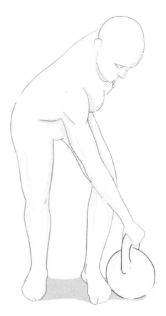

HOW TO TRAIN THE WALK?

For beginners, farmer's walk training involves more than simply adding weight like crazy. A broader view lies in the variation of load and distances.

Start with light weights and gradually progress to heavier weights as you progress. The initial structure of the programme includes sets of 8, 6 and 4 steps performed as SLOWLY AND CONTROLLED AS POSSIBLE, with full rests between sets.

The goal is to increase stability and control in a progressive manner, while maintaining a controlled and balanced speed. Once you have mastered the basic progressions, you can include more advanced protocols.

Advanced waves

Based on the spinal 'waves' exercise, we can add some variations that will allow us to take the stimuli of this exercise further.

We can start by performing the basic waves learned earlier. When the wave reaches approximately the first dorsal vertebrae, we continue the movement both through the neck and through the shoulders, elbows and hands. In this way, the 'wave' will be expressed from the spine to the movement of the arms, as if the arms were the final consequence of the movement of the spine. This action has no defined form, so feel comfortable exploring how the arms extend forward through the continuity of the wave that started in the spine. This is a way of integrating the movement of the wave with the arms in a continuous and coordinated way.

Experiment with different speeds and amplitudes of movement to see how this affects the feel and expression of the wave in your body. It is essential to maintain a fluid connection between the spine and the arms, allowing the movement to spread naturally and effortlessly throughout your body.

You can also perform the original wave, or this extended version with the arms, adding other movements and directions. For example, you can perform the movement not only forwards, but also forwards and a little to the right or to the left, thus adding a slight and subtle rotation to the movement. Sometimes you can go to one side and sometimes to the other, or combine one and one continuously. In this way, the whole wave will gain different planes of movement and allow you to perform combined movements, such as flexion/extension of sections of the spine with slight rotations. It is a good idea to build up the exercise by prioritizing the coordination issues first and then try to execute it with as little effort as possible and as much continuity and fluidity as possible.

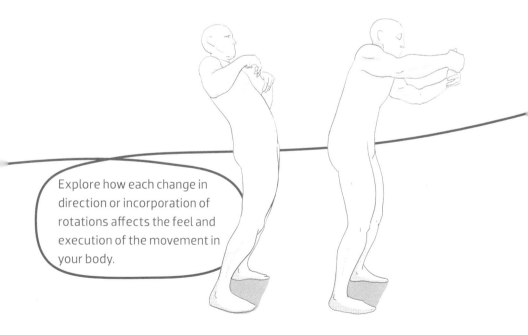

Explore how each change in direction or incorporation of rotations affects the feel and execution of the movement in your body.

Dancing with the cervicals

Always in a natural and comfortable situation, we will try to perform the following movements with our head, trying to keep our gaze level. This means that the height of our gaze will not change upwards or downwards during the following movements:

First, we will seek to spatially move the head forward. But remember, without modifying the height of gaze; this will mean that the skull will go forward, but will not articulate upward or downward. From this position, you will feel that it is very natural to move backwards. This shifting action may feel more comfortable in one direction than the other. Try not to overlook these differences and simply try to improve and feel the movements balanced and smooth in both directions. At first, the forward and backward movements will probably feel the easiest to perform.

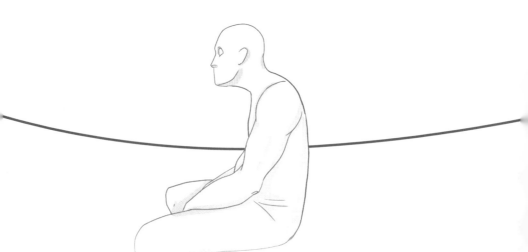

With this base, we can progress to more complex movements, such as lateral displacements. We keep the same instruction: the gaze is kept level as we move the skull to the right and then move it to the left. This can be done in a sectioned manner or more dynamically if we feel comfortable with the movement.

Finally, we can combine all the movements and perform a spatial displacement of the skull with circles to one side and then to the other, but always keeping the skull and eyes at the same level. These circular movements can be performed slowly at first and then increase the fluidity and range of motion as you feel more comfortable.

All these mobilizations will work specifically on the cervical spine, moving it in all its possibilities also activating the movement and circulation in all the structures that compose it, which we do not usually mobilize in conventional daily life. The key is to maintain smoothness and continuity of movement, without forcing or creating unnecessary tension in the neck or other areas.

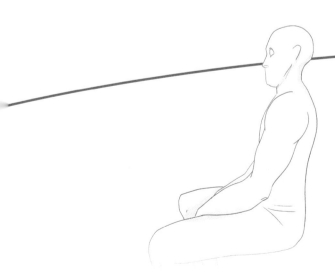

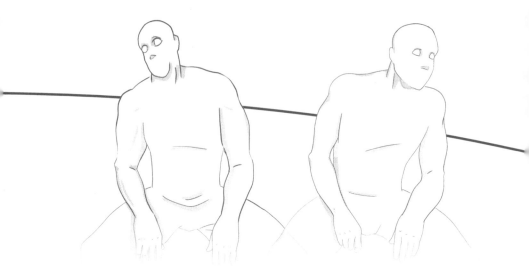

Generally, when talking about the cervical spine, actions such as 'make the least effort' are usually recommended, 'do not force' or 'move gently', due to the panic that this area can generate.

We have all suffered a contracture at some point and we know how annoying it can be. Unfortunately, this fragilizing attitude has led to a complete avoidance of working on neck strength.

If we usually strengthen our abdominals or the muscles that command the spine, why don't we do the same with the neck? To address this question, this book includes some simple exercises that you will see at the end of the book. It is important to note that neck strength training depends very much on the condition, possibilities, context and goals of each person.

Solo resources: small ball

We have noticed that, when we encounter perhaps discomfort or pain in the muscular structures surrounding the spine, pressure maintained on a point can sometimes relieve that discomfort. Pressure on an area can help relieve that area and there is also speculation that it can improve circulation after the pressure is removed.

Unfortunately, we do not always have a hand available and sometimes using our own hands can be uncomfortable or tiring. So one of the many resources is to use a ball, neither too soft nor too rigid (it can be a tennis or baseball ball, which have a firm but not rigid consistency). With respect to the spine, we will use it on the tissues and muscles surrounding the spine, trying not to work ON the spine directly.

We can use our own weight to get the right pressure. We lie on our back and position the ball between our body and the floor. The weight of the trunk will serve to regulate the amount of pressure we want to work with. We will choose a point at our discretion, either because we feel discomfort, hardness, restriction or pain, and we will rest the ball on that area. There is no set time; only the time that you intuitively feel or that experience can give you, but try not to stay more than two minutes per posture. You will probably feel the pressure of the ball on the area begin to give way to the pain or point of discomfort. It is important that you manage the pressures so that you do not feel uncomfortable pain or create more tension and an adverse reaction from your body in the area. The sense of discomfort and pain should always be decreasing, not increasing.

You can work on the sides of the spine, identifying tender points in an ascending way, going up the whole side of the spine, as descending, or intercalated. For example, once on the side of the lumbar spine and then immediately on the other side, going up one level on the right side and repeating on the left, and then moving up more levels. You can complete the whole spine or work on specific parts.

You can start all this work with the ball in what would be the center of the back of the neck (approximately in the fossa that we had identified as the first cervical). There you will notice that the ball fits quite well, always making sure that it is not painful or extremely uncomfortable. The gentle pressure in this area will relax and loosen the structures, and also in many cases provide a feeling of relaxation and general tranquillity.

Programs

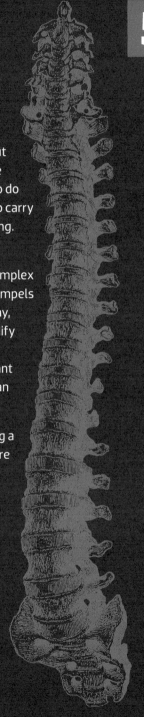

5

Ordering your bodily interventions is fundamental not only to keep an orderly record that you can compare but also to have a good mental predisposition PRIOR to the execution. It allows us to visualise what we are going to do BEFORE it happens and in this way we allow the mind to carry out its task in order to be better prepared for the training.

Programming can range from a simple reminder with crayons on paper, to a more organized diagram, to a complex spreadsheet. Everyone must find the way that most compels them to do it and that stimulates enthusiasm day by day, week by week and month by month to continue to modify and improve the plan to be carried out. There is no one 'model' that applies to everyone and it is VERY important that this process does not become more important than the action itself, which is to get the body moving.

While this plan may be held in your mind, I advise having a visual, or auditory or some kind of ACTUAL record where you can tangibly compare what you are planning with what actually happens.

It is very important that all these arrangements and expectations do not become a neurotic mechanism whereby the preparation and anxiety that might be generated by the design of a programme trumps the actual act of getting the body moving. Remember that these plans will allow you to compare what you envisioned in your mind with what actually happens.

¿Where?
¿When?
¿How much?

¿WHERE?

Sometimes it depends a lot on our context but also on our willingness or willpower available. We can have a dedicated area in our homes, it doesn't have to be a complete gym, sometimes a blanket or a dumbbell is enough. Don't let the environment condition you too much, the important thing is to move. Sometimes it can be the bathroom at work, a square, a corner in an airport or a fully equipped gym just for you. Exercises can also be adapted both in route, quantity and magnitude of the load.

¿WHEN?

It really can be at any time. It depends on what effect the exercise has on you and that's where we are all different. It can be in the morning, afternoon or evening. Even at a time when you can't get to sleep if the activity helps you get back to sleep. Remember that you can have anything from hour-long blocks to small training pills or snacks of a few minutes.

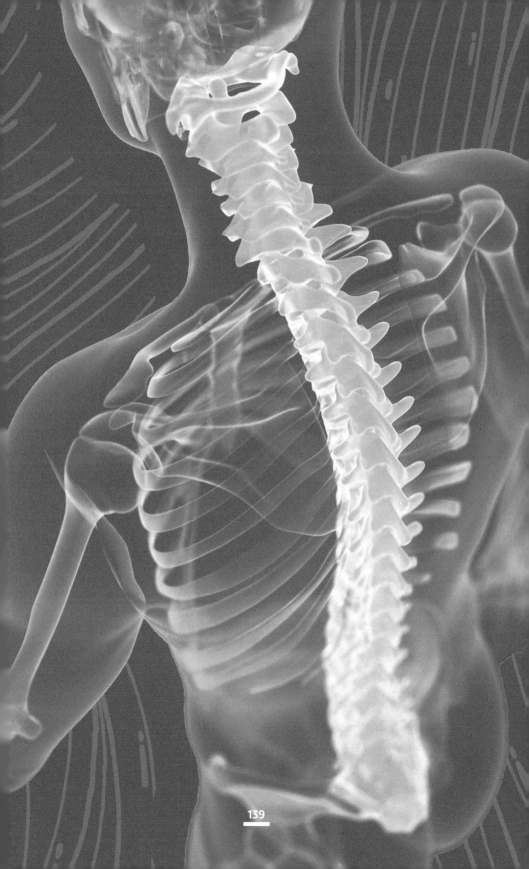

¿HOW MUCH?

This is perhaps the hardest question to answer ever because it will depend so much on the individual and their context. In other words: 10 repetitions of a low-load, low-impact exercise performed by an Olympic athlete is not the same as 10 repetitions for someone who has just come out of surgery. The 'how much' is going to depend first of all on your possibilities, your time and, very importantly, how you are and feel that day. Sometimes you can set an arbitrary number (e.g. 10 reps) not so much because that exact number will generate an adaptation in your system but because the number is conditioned by the time you have available or the amount of exercises you are looking to include in that workout. If it is a mobility exercise you can either set an arbitrary number that allows you to include it in your sequences and accommodate your times and other exercises, or you can choose a number where you FEEL that the exercise stimulated the tissues you were looking for and didn't leave you completely exhausted or sore. For some exercises such as strength training, a good recommendation is to look for a number that is close to what is called 'failure'. The best predictor (i.e. the number that tells you that you are close to failure) being 2 or 3 reps prior to failure. The proximity to failure can often be perceived when the speed of execution of the movement begins to slow down noticeably.

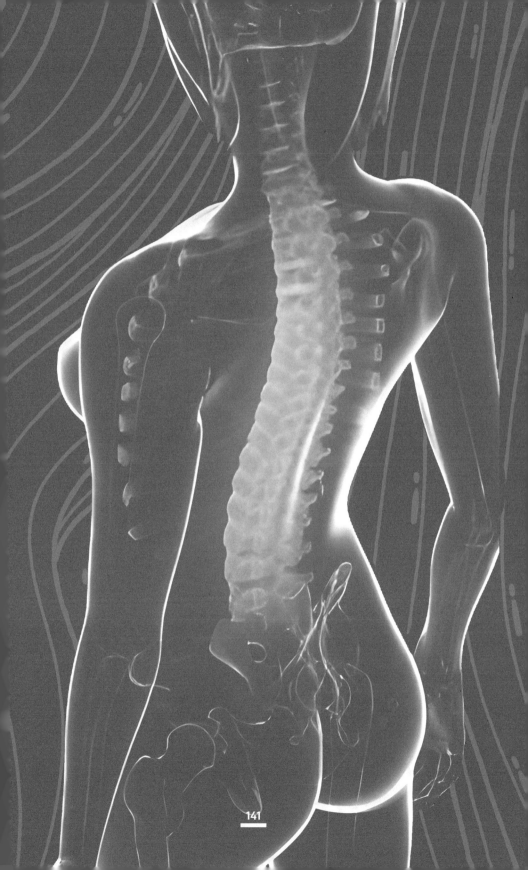

5-minute sets

A block of five minutes may seem like no time at all. But the reality is that in a busy, stressful day, it can be a real oasis for the mind and body. In this little snack of movement, you can either take a complete tour of several capacities or you can focus on a single one:

30 seconds of Shake hands (P. 69)

30 seconds of Raise your heels (Page 70)

30 seconds of Expand the abdomen (P. 71)

30 seconds of Pushing the sky (Page 74)

30 seconds of Lateral Bend (Page 76)

30 seconds of Archer (Page 78)

30 seconds of 1 foot (Page 80)

30 seconds of Rotations (Page 82)

30 seconds of Rear Chain (Page 84)

30 seconds of Wave (Page 86)

Here are 10 exercises performed one after the other in just 5 minutes. Is it a brutal stimulus? No, of course not, but the sequence served as an activator and stimulator of movement and circulation.

In 5 minutes we can also do a Turkish get-up but starting from a standing position. Getting to the floor will allow us to do some other exercises on the floor and then we can join in again with the Turkish get-up. We can spend 2 and a half minutes on each side and with a simple left and right execution we will have spent our 5 minutes in a series of compound movements.

10-minute sets

1. We can perform one minute of each exercise in our block of 10 exercises (Page 69 to 86).

2. Two minutes of each exercise:

- **Cat-camel (Page 40)**
- **Waves from cat position (P. 41)**
- **4 planks of 20 seconds with 10 seconds rest (Page 109)**
- **Bird dog 4 repetitions of 15 seconds alternating (P. 109)**
- **Face up, spine recognition and visualization (Page 37)**

3. Combined:

- Three minutes of pushing the sky (P. 74)
- Three minutes of farmer's walk supporting the weight every 30 seconds (Page 127)
- Two minutes of waves (Page 86)
- Two minutes of forward bending (P. 84)

4. Combined:

- One minute of holding the sky (P. 74)
- One minute of lateral tilt (P. 76)
- One minute of rotations (P. 82)
- 3 minutes of pouch walking, changing hands every 30 seconds (P. 127) 30 seconds (Page 127)
- 4 minutes of ball on the floor (P. 135)

5. Combined:

- 3 minutes of arm shaking (Page 69)
- 3 minutes of raising the heels (Page 70)
- 4 minutes of waves in all directions (P. 131)

30-minute sets

Based on the examples on the previous pages, we have seen that it is very easy to combine some exercises. The only care you need to take is not to perform passive stretching exercises PRIOR to a strength or intense activation exercise afterwards. For strength exercises, you will need the muscles to be pre-activated and not dormant from excessive stretching. It is also not advisable to start these strength exercises excessively relaxed or distracted.

BLOCK 1

- 10 minutes of active mobility exercises such as: pushing the sky, or waves.
- 10 minutes of combined strength or stability exercises such as: planks, weighted walks or holding weights in different positions.
- 5 minutes of weight bearing mobility exercises such as hinges or 3D.
- 5 minutes of analytical back exercises: isolated local movements. movements.

BLOCK 2

- 5 minutes of mobility: waves.
- 10 minutes of the basic exercise pack.
- 5 minutes of Turkish get-up.
- 10 minutes of strength/stability: weight holding, weight walking, advanced exercises.

Example of set 1

Active Mobility

Combined Force

Mobility with loads

Analytical

Interspersed times during the day

Sometimes we don't have an ideal schedule and can't dedicate even the minimum amount of time to a training session. Or it just happens to be a time when our daily schedule doesn't really allow us to take training blocks. Or, on the contrary, we have an ideal schedule that we have time for and, in addition, we have free moments during the day. These moments can be from 2 minutes to 30 minutes, and this may make us think that they are not enough to inoculate a training stimulus, but this is not really the case if you manage to distribute them efficiently.

You can organise your working day in blocks of 30 minutes each. Between each of these blocks, spend 5 minutes doing a specific exercise. For example, in a 6-hour workday, you will have approximately 10 exercise intervals. You can use the 10 exercises (pages 69 to 86) as the blocks between your work periods. In this way, without realising it, you will have built almost an hour of training into your workday, and these exercises will also serve as active breaks between your work tasks.

Or maybe you are extremely busy and can do these interventions at the beginning and end of your day with a break in the middle. You can include 10 minutes at the beginning, 10 minutes as a big break and one at the end as 3 medium volume interventions. This may not be as ideal as the previous one (because of the final time achieved) but it will still be a powerful training 'snack'.

Or maybe you have no time at all and have to do these interventions on the sly at work, but remember that 1 minute of any of these activities is 100% compared to doing nothing. Sometimes the stimulation is not enough to produce a physical adaptation, but the spiritual revelation of at least 'having done it' is enough to add up to emotional stimulation.

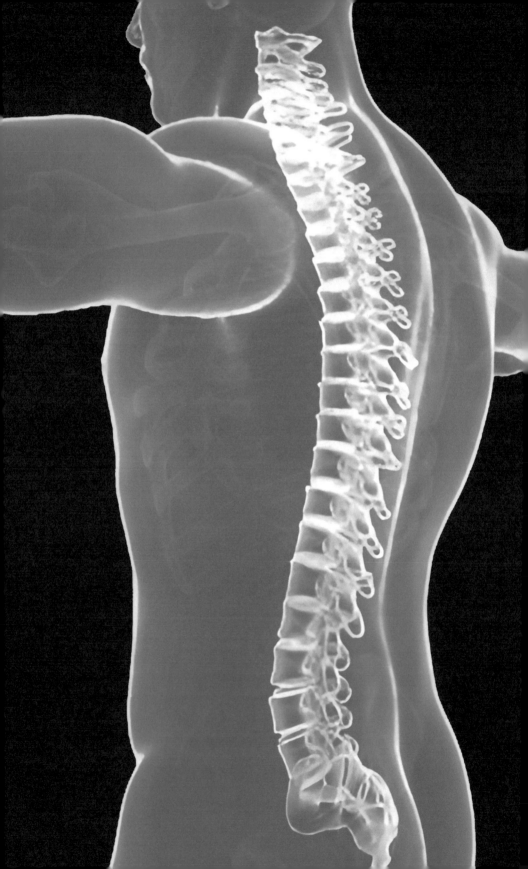

Advanced exercises

This chapter is considered 'special' and is not necessarily mandatory. It is recommended to perform these exercises only if you already have a strength base and understand the basic movement patterns, such as pulls, pushes, knee strength, hip strength, rotations and carries. These exercises require specific motor control, coordination and, above all, a training base and experience.

Strength training with weights has often been misunderstood and sometimes attributed with injuries or problems in the spine and other areas of the body. However, it is important to understand that we live in an environment where we need to use our strength to interact with external forces in the environment. For the vast majority of humans force management will be almost an inevitability.

In addition, strength training offers a number of benefits, including increased bone density, improved body composition, increased testosterone essential for muscle development, insulin regulation to prevent hormonal diseases and cortisol reduction helping to counteract the negative effects of stress on health.

ONLY approach this chapter if you already have a training base or if you can perform these exercises with the assistance of a professional trainer.

Care and warnings

When working with weights, the first important warning is not to attempt to lift a load that exceeds our capabilities in terms of tissues and structures. This may seem obvious and sensible, but most injuries that occur when working with weights are due to poor execution technique or the use of excessive loads.

Therefore, when working with overloads, it is essential to respect the following fundamental principles:

1. We should never increase the load abruptly. For example, if we are progressing from 2 to 4 kilos and then from 4 to 6, the next step should be 7 or 8 kilos instead of jumping straight to 10 kilos or more.

2. We should also gradually increase the number of repetitions and sets we perform in our exercises.

3. Intensity can be increased in a number of ways, such as performing the exercise with greater speed or increasing the range of motion.

It is important to note that we should try to increase only one of these three values at a time and not more than one at a time.

An additional important caveat is to take into account the person's current condition, weaknesses and sensitivities. If pain or discomfort is experienced when performing these exercises, it is essential to avoid them. Also, all exercises should be performed with a sense of safety and without pain.

Loaded mobility

Advanced exercises often combine strength and mobility into one, which requires coordination, motor control and certain basic skills, such as previous mobility and core strength. This makes them less suitable for the general public who are not used to this type of training.

Loaded mobility involves increasing joint range of motion while stretching a muscle while producing force with it, known as eccentric muscle action. Although it may sound counterintuitive to those unfamiliar, it is one of the ways the muscle can work, not only by shortening or avoiding movement, but also while stretching and trying to slow down an action.

WHAT IS AN ECCENTRIC CONTRACTION?

Eccentric muscle action refers to the moment when a muscle lengthens while it is working and producing tension (tension = force generated by contraction).

Imagine you are holding a spring at both ends and stretching it. As you stretch it, the spring lengthens, but you are still applying force to keep it stretched while the spring applies force to avoid being stretched. This is similar to what happens in muscles during eccentric activity. Even though the muscle is stretching, it is still working and applying force.

This is important because it allows the muscles to work in different ways and to control movements, even when they are stretching.

Hinges

The hip hinge movement has been the subject of criticism for decades due to concerns about its possible effect on the spine. However, it is a natural movement for humans and allows us to perform actions such as bending down to pick up objects from the floor or perform tasks in front of us.

The fundamental principle of hinge movements is that they should be managed primarily from the hips, with less involvement of the knees and ankles and avoiding significant changes in the position of the spine. This, of course, depends on the magnitude of the load being handled. For example, to lift a piece of paper off the floor and if you are in good health, you may not need to keep your spine completely straight. However, when it comes to more significant loads, it is recommended to keep the spine as neutral as possible.

To learn and improve hip hinge movements, you can start by lifting objects that are elevated to reduce the mobility demand on the hips. Over time reduce the height of the support.

Squats

The squat has historically been the subject of criticism due to unfounded fears that it may be harmful to the knees. However, in reality, if you are in good health and have no knee problems, the squat is a movement that is within the natural movement capabilities of our species.

The squat is a movement that not only allows you to bend down to pick up objects underneath you, but also to lift them. The principle of the squat is to execute the movement simultaneously and proportionally from the knees, hips and ankles. Within squats, there are different variations that may involve more action from the knees, the hips or a combination of both, and all of these variations are valid depending on the purpose you wish to accomplish.

In addition, the squat allows us to hold weights in different positions in relation to our body, either hanging, held in front of us, behind us and to the sides.

Windmill

The windmill is a multiplanar exercise and benefits the hip, shoulder and shoulder girdle. To perform it, imagine a dead weight (hip hinge) but with your feet in a diagonal direction.

This exercise works the glutes and the side of the thigh of the stretched lower limb. It is recommended to perform it without weights until you have a good technical mastery and then work with controlled weights, hanging, overhead or both at the same time.

- Stand with your feet in a diagonal direction according to your comfort and hip anatomy.

- Bend from the hips, leaning your torso forward. Although it may give the impression that you are also leaning laterally due to the position of your feet, remember that the lean is primarily forward, not lateral.

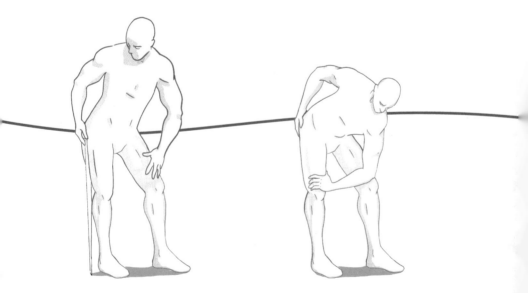

- When you reach the position of maximum flexion, extend one arm upwards while keeping the other arm downwards. This action will generate a natural rotation of the trunk, especially in the dorsal area.

- Make sure that the lowering hand remains centered between your feet. Prevent it from sliding to one side.

- During the exercise, maintain good technique and avoid sideways bending of the spine.

- Perform the exercise comfortably before including a load. No unusual discomfort or pain.

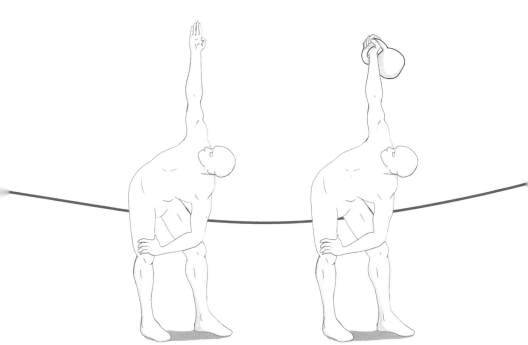

Depending on individual objectives, some exercises may be more suitable for certain functions than others:

Exercises for isolate a joint or a muscle (analytical):

- They allow a relatively smaller load to be moved.
- They are easier to learn.
- They allow localised strength and endurance work.
- They facilitate isolation and concentration on a single muscle.
- Can be useful for developing hypertrophy.

However, they lack specificity and have little transfer to functional or compound movements..

Exercises aimed at integrating more joints and muscle groups (compound exercises):

- They allow heavier weights to be lifted.
- Involve several muscles in a single exercise.
- They are more difficult to learn due to the coordinative complexity.
- Can be useful for developing hypertrophy.
- Require the use of additional stabilizers.
- Reduce isolated stress on a joint by allowing more weight to be carried by involving more muscles.
- Have good transfer and specificity to more functional and compound movements.

Analytical back exercises

Analytical exercises help us to focus on developing specific areas of our body either to stimulate a particular segment in need of improvement or for specific functional or aesthetic purposes.

Although spinal stabilization does not depend exclusively on the posterior musculature, we have seen many exercises that involve all parts of the trunk in a comprehensive manner. Now it is time to address the specific sectors of the posterior spine.

An example of a specific exercise is the 'trunk extension'. You can start by lying on the floor face down, slightly raising your head while extending your spine. This exercise can be performed from a safer position, which involves little extension of the spine but a lot of muscle activity (such as hanging while maintaining spinal neutrality in a static manner), to positions of greater extension. In both positions, the musculature is engaged, but the amount of spinal extension varies.

This extension can be performed on the whole spine or in more specific sectors such as the lumbar, dorsal or cervical area.

It is important to note that any extension of the spine beyond the neutral position also places increased pressure on the intervertebral discs. This is not necessarily detrimental, but it is a factor to consider, especially if a person has tenderness in these structures. Therefore, it is important to tailor spinal extension exercises to the individual's needs and comfort.

Spinal extensions, including those performed with moderate loads, can be beneficial for developing strength in the back musculature and working on spinal extension. However, it is essential to perform this type of exercise in a controlled and progressive manner.

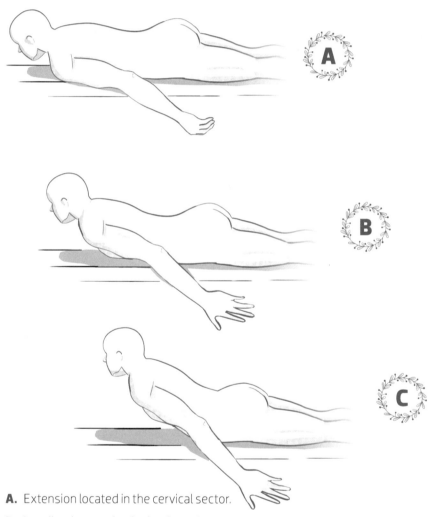

A. Extension located in the cervical sector.

B. Localised extension in the thoracic sector.

C. Localised extension in the lumbar sector.

Analytical exercises, such as classic crunches or lateral abdominal wall exercises, can also be useful for working the abdominal and back muscles. In these it is important to focus on producing movement in the spine and not so much in the hips.

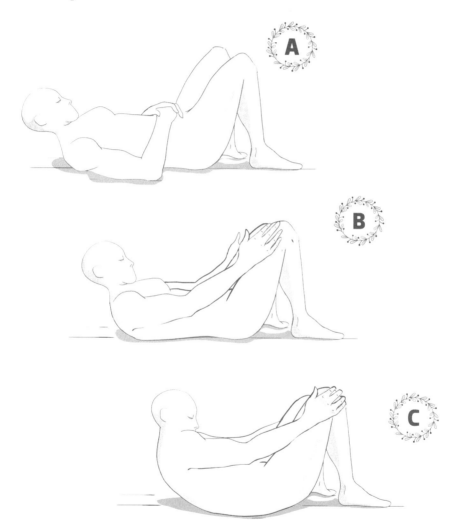

A. Localised flexion in the cervical sector.

B. Localised flexion in the thoracic sector.

C. Localised flexion in the lumbar sector.

Head and/or neck weights?

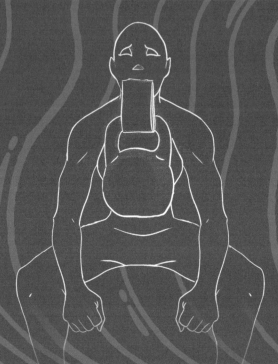

It is important to note that the cervical area can also be trained, but due to its structural differences from the rest of the spine, it is recommended to do so under the supervision of a competent professional. Historically, neck training with weights has been used by wrestlers, boxers, car racers and those who need to protect or build strength in this area.

Strength training of the neck can provide benefits such as increased muscle activity, safety and improved blood supply to the area.

Working the neck with overloads (either with weights or by supporting the head and using one's own body weight) is only suggested for people at an advanced stage of training, who have a specific developmental need in this area and who do not have neck injuries or sensitivities that could be affected by movement or loads.

These same spinal extensions and other movements can also be performed in a standing position and with the help of an external resistance such as an elastic band or weight. These movements can also be combined with extensions and rotations, bends and flexions with rotations, always bearing in mind that the sum of movements adds load and stimulation on a specific section of the spine, which for some people may be inconvenient.

Important in analytical exercises

- Repetitions are not carved in stone. If you are working with light weights and your body is already adapted, you could perform between 8 and 15 repetitions. Always start your progression with 2 to 5 reps.

- It is not advisable to train with weights that exceed the capabilities of your tissues and structures.

- We consider the unloaded exercises (1 and 2) to be fundamental for everyone else. For someone simply looking to maintain their fitness, these two would be sufficient.

- Exercises 3, 4 and 5 require good preparation, absence of pain, knowledge of the body and possibly the assistance of a professional.

- Exercise 6 is reserved only for completely healthy people with a thorough knowledge of the body and weight training.

1

Neutral without producing movement.
Maintain posture and avoid
movement.

2

Active extensions. Lifting and
lowering.

3

With band resisting flexion while
keeping the spine neutral.

4

With band generating
extension in the spine.

5

Holding a load but keeping the spine
neutral.

6

Extending the column with
loads.

Avoid extension in a neutral posture.

Flexing the spine dynamically.

Avoiding extension in front of a band
by remaining neutral.

Bend dynamically
the spine in front of a band.

Keep neutral by avoiding
extension under load.

Flexing dynamically
under load.

Compounds with the whole column

A comprehensive way to strengthen all sectors related to the spine is through compound exercises involving combined muscle contractions and stretching. These exercises do not allow for handling large loads due to the position of the spine in certain movements, nor do they focus on isolating specific muscles. Instead, they focus on combined movement chains to improve autonomy and functionality.

We can work them by first holding without a load to master the movement and then with a dumbbell that we can grip with one hand and allow us to hold it for moments with both hands.

1a. Backward extension with weight to the chest and Good Morning (anterior and posterior muscle chain).

We hold the load with both hands on our chest. From this position, we seek to extend backward forming a smooth arc with the spine and lower limbs. It is important that the movement does not occur in a single particular hinge of the spine, but that each vertebra contributes in a global sum that forms an arc. Next, we lean forward flexing mainly from the hips and slightly from the knees, until we feel the tissues at the back of the thigh slowing us down. At this point, we complete the forward hinge and can repeat the backward extension from this position.

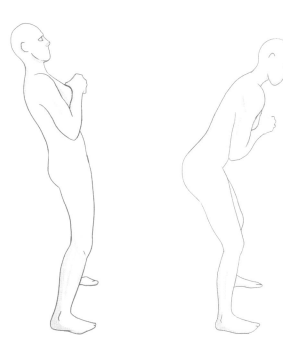

1b. (Advanced version) Backward extension with Pull and Jefferson Curl.

In this more advanced version we will try to hold the weight behind us hanging and when we go forward we will try to gently flex the entire spine to hold the weight in front and below us. This version is only suitable for people who have a good previous training and who do not present sensitivity with pain to the extension or flexion of the spine.

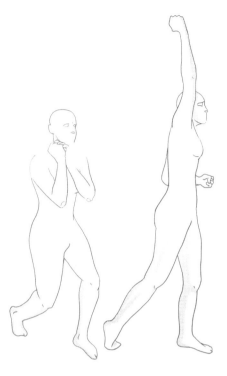

2. Unilateral thrust (ipsilateral muscle chain)

We hold the load near or over one shoulder with the same foot behind, keeping a flexion in that leg as if it were a compressed spring. From that position, we extend our legs while raising our arm to push the load over our head. We then return to the starting position and repeat the movement before changing sides.

BAREFOOT AND WITH LITTLE CLOTHING...

Practicing barefoot, along with wearing little or no clothing, offers a number of benefits. It stimulates sensory receptors in the feet, improving proprioception and stability. In addition, wearing little or no clothing provides greater freedom of movement and ventilation, avoiding unnecessary restrictions.

This combination strengthens the intrinsic muscles of the foot, improves the biomechanics of movement and promotes better circulation. By practicing barefoot and with little clothing, a greater connection to the ground is established and better body awareness is developed, which can facilitate balance and the execution of precise movements in some people.

3. From side to side (lateral muscle chain)

We start standing with the load supported or close to one shoulder. We bring the opposite foot behind the foot that is holding the weight. With this crossed posture, we lean towards the side where we have the load. Then, we return to the starting position and repeat on the other side with the same technique. We try to lean into the weight in a controlled manner, without being completely passive. We try to make the whole side of the body arch in a balanced way, avoiding excessive loads on a specific point.

4. Diagonal chop
(spiral chain and functional chains)

We begin by holding the load close to or over one shoulder with both hands, with the leg on the same side forward while in a slow, controlled movement, moving the shoulder away from the opposite hip. We then walk forward with the opposite foot and perform a diagonal forward cut, bringing the load as close to the opposite hip as possible. We then step back to bring the load back to the starting shoulder, and can perform this exercise in the same place as those two steps or in a walking format. Then, we change the weight to the other hand and repeat the exercise on the opposite side.

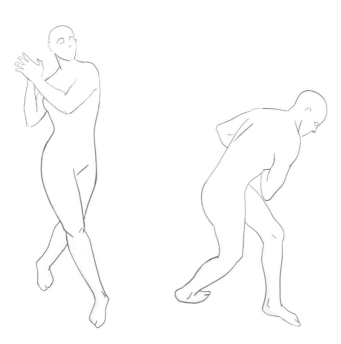

A thousand ways to keep your spine autonomous

Whenever you encounter restrictions, injuries or difficulties to recover movement on your own, there are ordered methods, such as Kinesiology, Feldenkrais, Osteopathy, Rolfing, Eutony, RPG, Pilates, and so on. I am not the one to determine which is the most convenient, you have to find which ones are more suitable for your system and way of being.

The exercises and concepts presented in this manual are not necessarily the absolute and only ones to keep your spine autonomous, but they have been an excellent example of a comprehensive and unifying program. There is a world of disciplines that can help you meet your goals. You can find methods such as functional training or specifically strength training, such as powerlifting, crossfit, weightlifting and bodybuilding, that will allow you to handle loads and use strength in different situations and contexts.

Body expression can also help to achieve this connection between mind and body, such as dance, theater and any system that seeks to link the mind with the body.

If your concern is interacting with outside forces and "real life situations", martial arts, whether traditional or modern, and combat sports such as Judo, Aikido, Karate, Kung Fu, Wrestling, Jiu-Jitsu, Submission and MMA are some of the many options available.

Epilogue

Understanding the concepts of some disciplines and what has been seen in this book will reveal to you that there really is no one truth, but infinite truths that coexist. And they are all fun to train in. Your task is to find how to navigate between them until you find your own way.

I hope that all these ideas have stimulated you to make movement as common and a priority in your life as breathing, drinking water or resting.

As I said at the beginning, this is not a book of recipes or magic formulas. It is a book that aims to awaken the enthusiasm to take back control of your body or to maintain that power every day.

YOUR BACK IS YOURS, ITS
STATUS MAY DEPEND ON YOU.
YOUR LIFE IS YOURS AND IT CAN
ALSO DEPEND ON YOU.

While it sounds like an arduous task to
accomplish, it is also the most wonderfully
empowering thing in life.

Bibliography

1. Boyle, Michael (2010). *Advances in functional training*. On Target. California.

2. Calais-Germain (2007). *Anatomy of movement*. Eastland Press. Seattle.

3. Cailliet, Rene (2004). *Biomecánica*. Marban. Spain.

4. Chia, Mantak. *Chi Kung - Camisa de hierro*. Sirio.

5. Contreras, Bret (2019). *Glute Lab: The Art and Science of Strength and Physique Training*. Victory Belt.

6. Di Santo, Mario (2012). *Amplitud de movimiento*. Paidotribo. Barcelona.

7. Franklin, Eric. *Dynamic alignment through imagery*. Human Kinetics.

8. Greenman, Philip E. (2005). *Principios y práctica de la medicina manual*. Panamericana. Argentina.

9. Guedes, Milo, Costa (2018). *Manual de caminata del granjero*. Edición propia. Buenos Aires.

10. Hainaut, Karl (1976). *Introducción a la biomecánica*. Jims.

11. Hamill, Joseph (2015). *Biomecánica bases del movimiento humano*. Wolters Kluwer. Philadelphia.

12. Horschig, Aaron (2016). *The Squat Bible*. Squat University LLC.

13. Janda, Vladimír (1983). *Muscle function testing*. Butterworths. UK.

14. Kapandji, A.I. (2008). *Fisiología articular*. Panamericana. Madrid.

15. Kendall, Florence (2007). *Kendall's músculos, pruebas funcionales, postura y dolor*. 5° Ed. Marban. Spain.

16. Lam, Kam Chuen. *Chi Kung, way of power*. Gaia Books Limited.

17. Levangie, Pamela (2005). *Joint structure and function*. F.A. Davis Company. USA.

18. Lieberman, Daniel E. (2012). *Those feet in ancient times*. Nature Vol. 483.

19. Lieberman, Daniel (2014). *The story of human body*.

20. McGill, Stuart (2007). *Low Back Disorders*. Human Kinetics. USA.

21. McGill, Stuart (2014). *Ultimate Back Fitness and Performance*. Backfitpro. Ontario.

22. Milo, Jerónimo (2020). *Kettlebells edición definitiva*. JMILO ediciones. Buenos Aires.

23. Miller, Cartmell. *Xing Yi Health Maintenance and Internal Strength Development*. High View.

24. Morris, Desmond. *El hombre al desnudo*. Círculo de lectores.

25. Myers, Thomas (2014). *Anatomy trains*. Elsevier. China.

26. Nordin, M. & Frankel, V.H. (2001). *Basic biomechanics of the musculoskeletal system*. Lippincott Williams & Wilkins. USA.

27. Rasch, Philip J. (1991). *Kinesiología y anatomía aplicada*. El Ateneo. Buenos Aires.

28. Rippetoe, Mark (2017). *Starting Strength*. Aasgaard. Texas.

29. Rouviere-Delmas (2005). *Anatomía Humana Descriptiva, topográfica y funcional*. 11° Ed. Elsevier.

30. Sagan, Carl. *Cosmos*. Planeta.

31. Schoenfeld, Brad J. (2020). *Science and Development of Muscle Hypertrophy*. Human Kinetics.

32. Sun, Lu Tang. *The study of Form-Mind Boxing*. High View.

33. Tohei, Koichi. *Aikido, su arte y técnica*. Glem.

34. Tsatsouline, Pavel. *Relax into stretch*. Dragon Door Publications.

35. Tsatsouline, Pavel. *Super Joints*. Advanced Fitness Solutions.

36. Yang Jwing, Ming. *Back Pain*. Ymaa publication.

37. Yang Jwing, Ming. *La raíz del Chi Kung Chino*. Sirio.

Made in the USA
Columbia, SC
14 February 2025

53855652R00100